The Life of
FAITH

D0369806

Mrs. C. Nuzum

GOSPEL PUBLISHING HOUSE
Springfield, MO 65802-1894

02-0539

18th Printing 2009

International Standard Book Number 0-88243-539-8

Printed in the United States of America

IT IS A WONDERFUL LIFE—THE
LIFE PICTURED IN THESE
PAGES—AND, BEST OF ALL, THE
READER IS SHOWN HOW
TO ATTAIN IT.

THIS
BOOK IS EARNESTLY
DEDICATED TO THE LOST SOULS WHOM
JESUS DIED TO SAVE AND TO HIS BLOOD-
BOUGHT SHEEP BY THE FEEDING
OF WHOM OUR FAITH
IS TESTED

Contents

Foreword

The author of this book was for years a missionary to the Mexican people, and amid the hardships and the hours of struggling to master both the language and the problems which arose continually, she learned the priceless art of expressing her thought in the fewest and simplest words. Thus she has become a writer of recognized merit. Her tracts have gone into many countries, and by them souls have been wooed and won to the Master, into whose image and likeness she is endeavoring to come. Reading these writings one can verily feel the impact of the Spirit, moving him into a new understanding of God's Word, and into the realization of a new relationship, in which he swings into touch with the Divine. The anointing of the Holy Spirit in these themes challenges each reader to come up higher, and to delve deeper into the mysteries of the kingdom, and pleads for lives of greater fruit-bearing. Throughout, the reader will be struck with the ease of expression and with a profound sense of the need of FAITH to carry him onward in the battle against the enemy. This need of faith is a constant call to greater strength, higher motives, humbler living, bolder witnessing, more purposeful striving, in the great program of God. Surely we shall be encouraged and have our hearts made glad in these perilous times when we read the thoughts of our dear sister based wholly upon the blessed Word of God.

ELMER FERGUSON MUIR

CHAPTER 1

"I Am Come That Ye Might Have Life"

A Testimony

I was born sick. My mother said that when I was a baby I cried most of the time. I never had any real childhood. While other children ran and played, I sat and talked to the older people. I had rheumatism all my life until the Lord healed me. My arm was so crippled that I could not put it back or up, but it is now free. My knee was so stiff that I could not straighten it, nor go up or down stairs. I can now run a block to catch a car, and my limbs are as supple as those of a girl of sixteen. My heart beat sometimes as though it would leave my body and at other times it seemed to stand still. Again it would tremble so it would cause a profuse perspiration. It pained me as though knives were being thrust through it. I can now go to the top of a mountain and not know I have a heart. I have been completely delivered from paralysis of the left side, and can now walk eight miles and feel fine the next day. I have been entirely delivered from constant fever and pain in the head, and from extreme nervous prostration. In my young womanhood, I was reported dead several times, and when I was graduated from school I had to sit down and rest while reading my thesis.

For twenty-seven years I was never one moment free from pain. I would gaze like a charmed bird at a healthy-looking face, and would gladly have given all that I owned if I could have felt for ten minutes as well people seemed to feel. My sufferings were such that I would rather have died than live. I was treated by the best doctors money could secure, and all concluded by saying the same thing, "There is not a sound spot in her to build health upon." My last doctor was a specialist who had been used to raise people from death's door to health. After a long, careful examination he said, "No doctor or medicine can cure you. You will have to die very soon. If you have any preparations to make, do it quickly."

What a shame to me that I had to be forced to take God as my physician instead of choosing Him. But, oh, how gracious He was to receive me and heal me, so that now at the age of seventy-one, I am doing the work of three women and have not lain in bed from sickness for so long that I cannot remember when I did so last. From having no strength, I have come to have the Lord's strength; from constant sickness to have His health; from forcing food just as I did the bitter medicine, I have come to have an excellent appetite, so that I can eat even the plainest food and enjoy it and never fail to eat a hearty meal, and every bite is sweet. Catarrh had destroyed my sense of smell. Now I can enjoy the perfume of the flowers. I wore glasses all the time. Now I use only a little reading glass, but thread my needle and sew without a glass. My sense of taste was so lost that both sugar and salt were as sand. Now, how good all food tastes! My hearing was so nearly gone that people were passing me before I heard them coming. Now I have ordinary hearing. For two years I scarcely slept at all; now I sleep like a baby. Then I could enjoy nothing; now I have the deepest enjoyment of all the things God gives me and especially Himself, His fellowship, communion, and Word. Truly, "old things are passed away; behold, all things are become new; and all things are of God." God did it all, and blessed be His name forever. I might add that I have worked strenuously three hundred and sixty-five days a year for thirteen years, with only two little vacations, and am in good condition now. When I look back at what I was, and see what I am, it seems incredible.

God protects as well as heals. I used to have a cold frequently. Now I go for years without a cold even when greatly exposed. I used to take every disease to which I was exposed. Now He keeps me from taking disease even when praying for the sick in close rooms, and when my hand is laid on those who have the most contagious diseases. Is not His name rightly called, "Wonderful"? My tongue cannot express the greatness of my deliverance, but my heart goes out to my great Deliverer in adoration, worship, praise, loyalty and thanksgiving. Who would not desire to be fully yielded to such an almighty, gracious loving One? My desire is to be one with Jesus in all things. How far we come short of this! How sweet are the words, "Conformed to the image of Christ." Oh, to so live that we may not hinder God, but let Him do this for each one of us.

CHAPTER 2

In Him Is Redemption

Are you redeemed? I suppose you would answer, "Yes." Well, from what are you redeemed? You answer, "From hell, from sin, from Satan, etc." That is true. All these are blessed parts of redemption; but are you redeemed in the full sense of the Word? Redeem means to buy back—to bring back to its former place. "Christ hath redeemed us from the curse," all of it, not some, nor even much of it, but *all* of it. Christ, the Redeemer, came to buy man back to the image of God, and to the place where He again walks and talks with God, and has none of the curse on him. Are you there? Does none of the curse cling to you? All that is not of life, health, strength, soundness, comfort, purity, and holiness, is of the curse. God says there is a place where the curse cannot come or stay—"Redemption . . . in Christ Jesus," and nowhere else. In Prov. 26:2 we read, "The curse causeless shall not come." Then, according to God's Word, if the curse, in any form or degree, clings to us there is a cause for it. To find the cause is necessary that we may be able to remedy it.

Prov 26:2

Does not the new birth put people in Christ? Yes, but hear God say, "As ye have therefore received Christ Jesus the Lord, so walk ye in Him." Col. 2:6. This is written to people who have been born again, who have received Christ. Why exhort them to walk in Him, if there be no danger that they will not do this? How often we are exhorted to abide in Him, and assured that we shall bear much fruit and have all our prayers answered if we abide in Him. But we are also told what it means to abide in Christ. "He that saith he abideth in Him ought himself also so to walk, even as He walked" (1 John 2:6)—live as He lived. "But," one may say, "man cannot live as the Son of God lived." Well, that is God's "high calling in Christ Jesus," and it is the only place where there is full redemption. God sent Jesus to show us how to live, and Jesus said, "Follow Me," which means to live as He lived. The Bible tells us that we are sent by the Lord as the Father sent Him, that we are to keep Jesus' commandments just as Jesus kept His Father's commandments.

We are to overcome just as Jesus overcame. We are not to be of the world, as truly as He was not of the world. In all things we are to follow His example, and we are told that He that sanctifieth and they that are sanctified are to be one, even as Jesus and His Father are one. Because people have thought this standard too high for them, and have not sought to attain to it, they have fallen short of full redemption. How seldom we find a child of God to whom some form of the curse is not clinging, but God says His people are to be without spot, wrinkle, or blame. Paul said, "Let us go on unto perfection." Heb. 6:1. Full redemption is perfection for spirit, soul, and body. The way to have this is to walk in Him. We are not merely to say that Jesus did it for us, but that Jesus will do it in us. If I sin by even a small transgression or neglect, therein I do not walk in Him, for "in Him is no sin." If I displease God, I am not then walking in Him. Jesus said, "For I do always those things that please Him." If I fail to obey, I do not walk in Him, for "He became obedient unto death." If I fail to love, I do not walk in Him, for "He is love." If I judge or condemn others I do not walk in Him, for He said, "I judge no man," and "Neither do I condemn thee." If I seek reputation, I do not walk in Him: "He made Himself of no reputation." He said, "I seek not honor from men. I seek not Mine own glory." "Even Christ pleased not Himself." He said, "I am meek and lowly." "He humbled Himself." "He answered not a word," even when they lied about Him and spoke evil of Him. He never resisted evil done to Himself, but let men do to Him as they chose. Can we say that we daily, hourly walk in Him in all these things? It is only in Him that we can have full, complete redemption.

Jesus said, "Without Me ye can do nothing," but the Bible also says, "I can do all things through Christ which strengtheneth me." Phil. 4:13. He always strengthens us to obey His commandments—so it is all of grace and He gets all the glory. In Psalm ninety-one, God tells us how He will protect, deliver, and work for those who abide in Him, those who make Him their habitation, their constant dwelling place. The ninth and tenth verses of this Psalm tell us that because of this full, perfect abiding in the Lord, He will let no evil befall us. Verse fourteen says He will deliver us; that means, He will set us free from all the curse, and set us on high above the power of Satan. He says He does this because we have known His name, and we can only know His name by living as He lived day by day. If any of the curse, whether it is disease, weakness, pain, sorrow, depression, or sadness, clings to us, it is because the old things are not all passed away, and we still live in some of the old things of the natural man instead of abiding in Christ.

God wants us to resist the devil and rise above temptation and live in daily victory through walking in Him. "Therefore if any man be in Christ ... old things are passed away"—we are no longer to live in them. 2 Cor. 5:17. It was on these old things that Satan could work, and while one of them is left, he can annoy us, but he can put nothing on Christ, nor on us as we fully abide in Him. "We know that whosoever is born of God sinneth not; but he that is begotten of God keepeth himself, and that wicked one toucheth him not." 1 John 5:18. "Put off the old man"; "put on the new man." "The name (what Christ is) of the Lord is a strong tower, the righteous runneth into it, and is safe." Prov. 18:10. "No evil shall befall thee." God will enable us to abide fully, wholly in Him, and remain there if we will set our wills to get there at any cost. "Thy people shall be willing in the day of Thy power" (Ps. 110:3), means that when you set your will to have God's whole will done constantly in you, He will put His mighty power back of your will and bring it to pass.

Ez 36: 26 I will give you a new heart and put a new spirit within you; I will take the heart of stone out of your flesh and give you a heart of flesh

CHAPTER 3

REMEMBER THY CREATOR

This is a positive command and therefore very important. But, why did not God say remember your keeper, provider, preserver, benefactor, or God? He is to us all these blessed names signify, but He bids us remember Him as Creator because we need to be created in Christ. One says—"I was created in Christ when I was born again." True, but have you all of Christ that you desire to have? Can you not see things in Christ that you lack? If you cannot, perhaps others do and by a careful, honest comparison of yourself with Christ, I believe you will find things in Him that you lack. God took great pains to tell us how He created natural things so that we might have great confidence in His creating in us the needed spiritual things.

He tells us how He just spoke the word and material things came into existence and He will do the same in spiritual things. When we first come to Christ, we have nothing in us like Him, but in the new birth God creates in us the nature of Christ. Ezekiel 36: 26 tells us He cleanses us, puts a new spirit and a new heart within us and a desire to obey God. But, as we go on we find people that are so different from all that we think they ought to be, that it seems impossible to love them. God commands us to love everybody and we long to obey, but the love for

18

them does not seem to be in us. "Remember thy Creator." The Creator does not have to have a love in you to work on. No, He makes love to exist where before there was none. Cry out to Him to create in you a real true love for that repulsive person; believe that He wants to be remembered as Creator and that He will now create love within you. You will be surprised to find how interested you become in that person and how you desire to do love services for him.

Has someone done you so great a wrong as to cause you loss and sufferings and does the memory of all you have borne press you so sorely that it seems impossible to fully forgive and forget and be as if the wrong had never been done? "Remember thy Creator." Cry out to Him in real faith and see how pity and compassion will rise up in your heart and see how the memory of the wrong will be swallowed up in a desire to help and better the offending one. Is there a lack of meekness, so that you rebel against undeserved criticism, talk back when falsely accused? Do you resist faultfinding and grumbling, and dislike? Do you resent slights, injuries, and evils thrust upon you, chafe under ingratitude and evil done you in return for the good you have done? "The Creator . . . fainteth not, neither is weary." Isa. 40:28. Ask Him to create in you Christ's meekness so that like Him you will not open your mouth nor resist a thing done to you, but like Him, pray God to forgive the doer. Is what you need a humility that will make you never desire to be seen or heard or known as one who is used of God, or who is able in prayer, testimony, teaching the word, or in holy living—glad to do and be these things, but having no desire to be known because of them? "Remember that the Almighty Creator" just waits and longs to create this also in you and can do it, even if you have had great pride because of all these things. "He taketh away the first that He may establish the second."

Is it a spirit of prayer and communion, or a spirit of praise and worship, or a spirit of intercession and supplication, or a passion for lost souls, of which you stand in need? "Remember thy Creator." Hear Him say, "Created unto good works," that we should "walk therein." Do you desire to speak for Him? He says, "I create the fruit of the lips." Isa. 57:19. No matter what your lack, shortage, or need is, the great Creator stands ready, able and willing—yea more—He longs to create in you whatever you need to make you like Christ and an able, successful worker for Him. "My God _shall_ supply all your need," and it is so easy for Him to create within you all that will fit you to be what Jesus was and to do the works He did. But remember the new spiritual creation is "created _in_ Christ Jesus." We must obey—"looking unto Jesus" until we see what we need in Him. God gave Him to us and chose us _in_ Him. We must by an act of faith "run into His name" (this thing that is in Him), know we are _in_ it, for no other reason than that we ran into it by an act of faith; ask no proof of sight or feeling, but just stand still in that thing; ask and believe that "Our Creator" _is now_ creating that thing in us.

Wait at His feet knowing that He is creating, because "He worketh for him that waiteth" and He also "worketh while he waiteth." How God loves to create us in Christ, because He gets more glory out of this second creation than He did out of the first. After waiting in praise and worship while God creates, rise and act what you have taken and you will find that God has truly created in you all you really believe He has created.

CHAPTER 4

LAY THEM ASIDE

In Heb. 12:1, God tells us to lay aside weights and sin. Jesus bore them all for us and truly loosed us from them but Satan put them on us in the first place and he will try to hold them on us and press us into using and serving them after we are freed.

When we lay aside an article, we put it away from us. It may have been on us or in our pathway, but we put it away from us.

A weight is something that makes it harder for us to move along well and rapidly—holds us back from good and easy progress. We may possibly move on with it, but not so well or so fast or so far as if we did not have it.

Possessions may be a weight. God says—"How hardly shall they that have riches enter into the kingdom?" Luke 18:24. How much better to use the riches for God and get great reward and make it easier to enter in! Cares may be a weight. "The cares of this life" choke out the things of God and so God says, "casting *all* your cares upon Him."

Much business may be a weight. Labor not for the meat that perisheth, but labor for that meat which endureth unto life eternal. "He that provideth not for his own household ... is worse than an infidel." "But having food and raiment, let us be therewith content." 1 Tim. 6:8. Having our minds occupied with things of

22

time and of this life may be a weight. "Transformed by the renewing of your minds." "Thou wilt keep him . . . whose mind is stayed on Thee." An unwillingness to suffer may be a weight. "If we suffer, we shall also reign with Him." Old habits may be a weight. "Raised up from the dead . . . walk in newness of life." Rom. 6:4. Self-will may be a weight. Jesus said, "I delight to do Thy will, O God." A desire to be seen and heard may be a weight. "Ye are dead and your life is hid." A desire to be the leader may be a weight. "Neither as being lords over God's heritage." "All ye are brethren." "Take the lowest room." Jesus washed feet. A desire to be honored may be a weight. Jesus said, "I seek not Mine own honor." It may be a desire to have others hear how God has used you. Jesus said, "The words I do, these bear witness of Me." A desire for position, attention or esteem may be a weight. "He that humbleth himself shall be exalted." "He giveth grace to the humble." "Humble yourselves in the sight of the Lord and He shall lift you up." James 4:10.

Timidity may be a weight. "The righteous are as bold as a lion." Sensitiveness may be a weight. Someone has said true humility is entire forgetfulness of self. Your weight may be a man-fearing spirit. "Be not afraid of their faces." It may be self-love. "Let him deny himself." Mark 8:34. It may be love of pleasure. "She that liveth in pleasure is dead while she liveth." 1 Tim. 5:6. It may be a love of comfort. "Endure hardness." It may be a love of ease. "Take up the cross and follow Me." Self-sufficiency may be a weight. "Our sufficiency is of Christ." Your weight may be fear. "I will trust in the Lord and not be afraid." It may be unbelief. "Faithful is He that calleth you who will also do it." It may be a hard heart. "I will take away the stony heart." It may be weakness. "Take hold of My strength." It may be pride. "Humble yourselves under the mighty hand of God."

God's children have put away great sins, but maybe there are smaller sins that God is calling you to lay aside. Do you ever judge? "Thou art inexcusable, O man, whosoever thou art that judgeth." It is sad to do a thing God tells us He will not excuse. Maybe your weight is criticising. Jesus said, "He that is without sin among you, let him first cast a stone at her." John 8:7. Who among us can say, "I never sin in thought, word or deed"? Then, we are not to condemn others any more than were they to throw a stone at the woman. Is faultfinding our weight? God says, "Charity covers the multitude of sins." 1 Peter 4:8. When they are covered you cannot see them. Do we murmur? God says, "Neither murmur ye as some of them also murmured and were destroyed." 1 Cor. 10: 10. Something about us is always destroyed when we murmur—it may be fellowship or communion with God; it may be health, strength or joy—something will surely be destroyed for God said so. Have we a grudge against anyone who has wronged us? God says, "Grudge not." James 5:9. Is thinking or speaking evil of someone our weight? Love "thinketh no evil." 1 Cor. 13:5. "Speak evil of no man." Tit. 3:2. God tells us to lay these things aside, and we do so by refusing to see them, to think of them, or to use them.

If we had a broken chair that someone might sit in and get hurt by a fall, we would be careful to put it where no one would ever sit in it, and would put a good chair in its place.

Hear God say, "Put off the old man with his deeds." Col. 3:9. Lay these things aside. They are of the old man. God says, "Put off the old man with his deeds," and we do it by refusing to obey or serve him, or even to listen to or recognize him. We put on the new man by fully obeying the Word, following Jesus, walking in Him, and walking as He walked.

CHAPTER 5

A Pure and Holy Life

No life is pure and holy unless it is like Christ's life. As we look at the Scriptures we see that God expects us to live a pure and holy life. We realize that we cannot live it in our own strength, but God says in Isa. 27:5, "Take hold of My strength," and in Isa. 49:5, "My God shall be my strength." 2 Cor. 12:9 says, "My strength is made perfect in weakness." In His strength we can put self, the flesh, and all the carnal nature down and out of our lives and continue to do so; and, as we do this, Christ holds sway in our lives, and, of course, when He rules supreme upon the throne of our hearts we will live Him out in our thoughts, words, and actions. 1 John 4:17 says, "As He (Christ) is, so are we in this world." He took all of us, and it is only as we forsake all of ourselves in an exchange for all of Christ that it is possible for us to live this pure and holy life. We never get *all* of Christ unless we forsake *all* of self.

Jesus became what you were, and the Bible tells us that it was so that you might become just what He is. 2 Cor. 5:21. He took our nature so fully that He could be, "in all points tempted like as we are." Heb. 4:15. We are to have His nature so that we cannot be tempted sufficiently to make us yield to temptation. He took our fallen nature, that was subject to all the curse, in order that we might have His divine nature which can resist all the curse. He took our weaknesses

Exchange !

in order that we might have His strength. He took our humanity that we might be filled with His divinity. "Partakers of the divine nature." 2 Peter 1:4. He took our impatience that we might have His patience. He took our hate that we might have His love. He who was always meek, took our pride that we might have His humility.

He took our nature—which resists all evil done to us—in order that we might have His meekness, and so obey God, not resisting evil, but bearing with joyfulness all the evil that God *permits* people to do to us. He, who did all His Father's will, took our disobedient spirit in order that we may have His obedient spirit—a spirit which delights to do the will of God, even when there is great suffering connected with it. He took our hasty spirit in order that we may have His long-suffering spirit, ready to suffer all things, even when long continued, and still be kind. He took our sicknesses in order that we might have His health. He took our pains that we might have His freedom from pain. He took our poverty of life that we might have the abundant life that He came to bring, so that our whole spirit, soul and body can be preserved blameless. He became so poor that He had not where to lay His head in order that we may lack nothing, and says, "My God shall supply all your need." Phil. 4:19. He took our banishment from God that we might have continual fellowship with God. He became our sin that we might become His holiness. He became our unrighteousness that by faith we might be perfectly righteous.

Jesus chose to take upon Himself, and really, be, all the things that we were, and God let Him take

His place thus and make Him to be those things.
Although He was not at all like any of them, but
because He chose to be so, and never turned away
or let them go God made Him really to be them. His
one purpose in doing all this was to make it possible
for us to have everything that He is—being and abiding in us. Just as Jesus chose what we were, so we
must choose to be exactly what He is, and no more
let go or turn away than Jesus did. God is just as
willing to let us have all that is in Jesus as He was
to let Jesus have what was in us. He gets great
glory when we take Jesus' place. Jesus never once
stepped back into Himself, into the greatness and glory
which were His before He took our place. God says
to you, *"Deny yourself,"* and He means you are to
live as entirely separate from your self-life as Christ
lived separate from His heavenly life. He never once
went back to enjoy that life even for a little while.
You must never step back to live and enjoy your
old life even for a little while. When Jesus died you
died. Death is separation, and your death in Christ
separated you from *all* your old evil things.

Satan will come and bring you some evil things and
he has the power to make you feel them, and tries
to make you believe they are the same old things you
used to have. They are not. Tell Satan that Jesus
separated you from these old things and that you
refuse to have these from Satan, because God says,
"Neither give place to the devil." Tell Satan you
have the opposite of that evil thing and that you
got it from Jesus. If Satan tries to make you feel
angry at someone, tell him Jesus separated you from
all such anger and that you have nothing but Jesus'

love in its place. If Satan tries to make you resist the evil that people do to you, tell him Jesus took away your spirit of resisting the evil done to you, and that you have Jesus' spirit of doing good in return for every wrong done unto you. If Satan tries to make you judge and criticize someone, tell him Jesus separated you from all that, and gave you His Spirit. He says, "I judge no man." He said, "I do always those things that please Him." If Satan tries to get you to do things to please yourself, tell him Jesus separated you from that and gave you the Spirit of Christ, who "pleased not Himself." If Satan tries to put sickness upon you, tell him Jesus separated you from sickness, disease, pain and weakness, and you have His health, strength, and freedom from pain.

It takes all these things to make one truly and fully pure and holy and righteous, because righteousness means "being right" and Jesus came to make us right in spirit, soul and body. Jesus has given us Himself. He *has* separated us by His death from all our evil things. When He said, "It is finished," He had done it all for us, and our part is to believe it is *done,* no matter how we feel or seem to be.

God says in effect, that, "His righteousness is imputed to all them who *believe.*" You must believe that you are separated from the old evil things, even if you feel them in all their power. You must believe you have the holy things of Christ in you, when you cannot find one of them. God's law to everybody is unchangeable and is "As thou hast *believed,* so be it done unto thee." Matt. 8:13. God never says He will make things as you *feel,* nor as you *seem,* nor does He even say that it shall be as you pray, but

He says many times that it shall be exactly as you believe. Faith and obedience are the two things that count with God. You get the things God offers you in the Bible by believing Jesus did all for you, purchased all for you, has given all to you, and makes it truly yours the moment you accept. You keep them by never doubting that you *have* them, though you have no reason for believing it, except that you accepted them as a gift from Jesus, and now have them because you accepted them. Then follows obedience. You must act just as one would who had them all. God says you must not let one of your members serve one of the old things of your former life, but see to it that every member is used for the new things that you have taken from Christ. Your faith causes you to have the things, and acting as though you had them causes you to keep them. God will make the things you believe Jesus separated you from, leave you entirely, as you refuse to let your members serve them, and He will make the things of Christ, which you believe you have and which you make your members serve, show themselves within you, so that you can be conscious of them and can fully enjoy them. This is what God calls "created in Christ Jesus." He makes the things of Jesus come into evidence and enjoyment. This is what He means by "If any man be in Christ Jesus he is a new creature: old things are passed away," because you refuse to use them. All things are new and these new things are of God. They are the things you took from Jesus by faith and keep because you believe you have them and use them. As you live in this way, God says "Sin *shall* not have dominion over you." Rom.

6:14. He means that as you believe and act in this way, God's mighty power will be with you to give you the victory every time. This is to claim for yourself all that Christ is for you now. "As He is so are we in this world." "To whom ye yield yourselves servants to obey, his servants ye are." Rom. 6:16.

You were no more like Jesus when you first came to Him than Jesus was like you when He took your place. God by His mighty power made Jesus become what He was not—even sin. Just so, as you take your place in Christ by faith, God says He accepts you in the Beloved and, as you obey God and put on Christ by acting just as He would act if He were in your place, God by His almighty power, will make you to be what you were not—even the righteousness of God. God did not force Jesus to become sin, but made Him to be sin, because He took His place there of His own will.

Just so, God will not make *you* to be righteous until you choose to be so, take your place by *faith,* and maintain your place by acting it—then God will make you to be righteous and holy as truly as He made Jesus to be sin. Then shall it be true, "For to me to live is Christ," reproduced. Also "Not I but Christ," and you close in with Christ who said He gave Himself for us. Then the Christ light will shine out through you wherever you go, and your life will do far more for God and for His kingdom than the best preaching that any mortal can do. Then will be true of you, "Ye are our epistles . . . known and read of all men." 2 Cor. 3:2. Then God will enable you to realize the words of Jesus, "The works that I do shall he do also,"—*all* of them. John 14:12.

Psalm 29:11 The Lord will give strength to His people

CHAPTER 6

STRENGTH

I find many people who lay hold of the Lord and get healing, but who remain weak and seem unable to get strength. Yet God has provided strength, and it is obtained from Him in the same way as healing—namely, by repentance, obedience and faith. "My God shall supply *all* your need," applies to strength as well as to healing, and He supplies it in the same way and with the same willingness—strength for spirit, soul, and body. Jesus bore our infirmities (weaknesses) as truly as He bore our diseases, and for the same purpose—that we might be freed from them. Because He bore them, we do not have to bear them. He does not want us to bear them, and is delighted when we rise up and refuse to bear them. "Neither give place to the devil," applies to weakness just as much as it applies to sin and sickness. Weakness is a part of the curse as truly as pain is, and "Christ *hath* redeemed us from the curse" (all of it); it is in the past tense—it is done. He is not only the Redeemer to buy us back from the curse, but also the Deliverer to set us free from it all, and longs to "see of the travail of His soul (the results of His sufferings) and be satisfied," because He sees that we have the benefits of it.

Psalm 29:11 says, "The Lord will give strength unto *His* people," but some of His people are not strong. 1 Cor. 6:20 commands us to glorify God in our bodies

Hand g faith

—a weak body does not glorify God. God created man in His own image, and "In the Lord...is strength," so weakness is a part of the curse that Jesus bore for us.

Christ delivered us from weakness at the same time He delivered us from sin. Again and again in the Bible we are commanded to "be strong." Another verse says, "The people that know their God shall be strong." Isaiah 27:5 says, "Let him take hold of My strength," and Acts 3:16 says faith in the name of Jesus made a man strong that had never been strong before in his life. That man came to know God, and took the strength of God—not natural strength, but God's strength—and got it by faith.

Just as the body has a hand of flesh that lays hold of material things, takes and holds fast to them, even so the spirit has a hand of faith that takes hold of the things God offers and holds fast to them. How often God begs us to take things. How shall we do it? The hand of flesh feels what it takes, but the hand of faith does not depend on the sense—it depends only on the Word of God. Did God give it and say, "Take it"? Then faith lays hold of it and *knows* it has it, not because, like the hand of flesh it feels what it has taken, but because the God who never mocks, deceives, or changes said, "Take it," and I did take it, and therefore I *do* have it, even though I cannot see, feel, or find it as yet.

Then God says, "Hold fast that thou hast" by never once doubting that you really have it. Then Joel 3:10 says, "Let the weak say, I am strong." Not the strong ones say, I am strong, but the weak ones. Not say, "I shall be strong," but "I *am* strong now." Not say

Isaiah 40:31
my strength is made
perfect in weakness

it after you get strong, but say it while you are weak. Of course, you must think it and believe it, but you must also *say* it, because Mark 11:23 says you shall have what you say if you doubt not, and Jesus said, "As thou hast believed, so be it done unto thee." So do both—believe it and say it also. As you thus obey God you will have the experience of Heb. 11:34—"Out of weakness were made strong." This is what Paul meant when he said, "When I am weak, then am I strong" —not his own strength increased, but his hand of faith "took hold of God's strength" and he had, as one translation gives it—"the strength of dynamite."

Psalm 41:3 says God will strengthen even on a bed of languishing. He also declares that "As thy days so shall thy strength be." If today is harder than yesterday, God has pledged me more strength—yea, sufficient strength for all my need. God says, "*My* strength (not your human strength) is made perfect in weakness." Isa. 40:31 says, "They that wait upon the Lord shall exchange (marginal for "renew") their strength." That means that they will give God their puny, little strength, or their utter weakness, and get in return His strength, because the Bible says He gives Himself for us—what a wondrous exchange! It is when we have exchanged our strength for His strength that Phil. 4:13 is true—"I can do all things through Christ which strengtheneth me."

God sees our great need of His strength and cries out, "Awake, awake, put on thy strength." When such a wonderful provision that we may have God's strength is put before us, God says surely we must be asleep, or we would rise up at once and lay hold of it.

When people are asleep, they see things but remain inactive, and that is what people are doing about this wonderful strength God offers them.

Psalm 84:7 says, "They go from strength to strength," showing there is no limit to the strength God will give. Weakness and weariness depart as you believe you have God's strength, rest and refreshment, not because you feel strong or rested, but because you took strength. But one says, "Jesus, Himself, was often weary, and we must not expect to be free from weariness." Yes, and Jesus was made to be sin, but it was that we might be free from sin. Jesus could not free us from anything unless He bore it in our place. He bore our sins, sicknesses, weaknesses, and wearinesses in order that we might be freed from them all. Jesus said, "I will give you rest," "Take my yoke . . . and ye shall find rest."

Why not take the rest God says He has given us the moment we feel the least weariness, instead of bearing the weariness awhile and then taking the rest? We take deliverance from sickness the moment it attacks us. Let us do the same with weariness and weakness. I pray for rest for people just the same as I do for healing, and if they believe, they get it. I have seen extreme weariness leave people as quickly and as fully as pain does, when by faith they took His rest, and have often experienced the same myself.

It was not that life of Jesus that He was born with, and that was subject to our weaknesses (because He "took upon Himself our nature") that He gave to us. No, He said He laid that life down. He gave to us the life that came to Him in the tomb, and God says He will work in us with the same mighty power with which He worked in Jesus when He raised Him from the dead if we will only believe for it, and it will work the same life in us that it worked in Jesus. Eph. 1:19, 20.

Weakness goes in the same way that you take His strength, by believing and acting your faith, by doing things before impossible to you. I have often left my room feeling too weak to begin the work, but as I took and believed I had His strength, I have worked hard all day and until ten at night, and retired feeling strong. But God says, "The fiery trial which *is* to try you." There is no escape from it, and it will be fiery —will hurt you. The weakness and weariness may seem greater—overpowering—but as you never waver, or doubt that you have His strength and rest, the weakness and weariness go, for God says everything shall bow at the name of Jesus, and you have stepped into that part of the name of Jesus, and what was of the natural has to go. "Made partakers of the divine nature." "The Lord is my strength," "I will give thee rest."

CHAPTER 7

HOLD FAST THAT WHICH THOU HAST

I find that many of God's children can get healing, but cannot keep it. The above words show that there will be a power arrayed against whatever God gives us. The words, "Hold Fast," indicate that it will not be easy to keep that which we take from God. Satan is arrayed against God and against all His work, and he endeavors to undo what God does, but the Bible says, "What God doeth, it shall be forever." All the evil that ever comes to us is from Satan.

When God gives deliverance, and drives the evil one out, the Word tells us that Satan will say, "I will return to my house from whence I came out"—that is, he will seek to return to the very place from which he was driven. It is God's will that he shall not return, even as it is God's highest will that Satan shall not harm us in the first place. We are all in the land of the enemy and are subject to his attacks in spirit, soul, and body, but God says, "Give no place to the devil." That means that he cannot take a place in us when he attacks us if we do not *let him. We* open the way for him to come in if we sin; the smallest sin we commit in word, deed, or thought, gives place for the devil to do us harm.

Jesus said, "The prince of this world cometh, and hath nothing in Me." And he could not harm Jesus. Our Saviour *took* upon Himself our sins and sicknesses and *laid down* His life. The devil did not have power to take Jesus' life, for He tells us that He laid it down of Himself. God entreats us to separate from all sin so that the enemy cannot touch us. "That evil one toucheth him (us) not."

We also let Satan have a place by submitting to him, but God tells us to "resist the devil," and declares that he will then flee. God gives us an invincible weapon, the all-powerful blood of Jesus. Jesus gave His own blood as a ransom and it is written, "They overcame him (Satan) by the blood of the Lamb, and by the word of their testimony." "This is the victory that overcometh . . . even your faith." So we see that it is the blood of Jesus, and faith in His shed blood, that always enable us to overcome the devil. The Blood robs him of all power to afflict us, if we will only hide away under it.

We read in the Bible that some were not benefited, because they did not mix faith with the Word. We must believe that God covers us with the Blood when we ask Him to do so, because Jesus said, "My blood is shed for you." We must also believe what God says about the blood of Jesus, that it overcomes Satan, takes all power from him. When we are covered with the Blood, Satan is powerless to enter, to put evil upon us. If the evil is already upon us, when the Blood is applied in faith, Satan loses his power to keep the evil there. "Whom resist steadfast in the faith." If the enemy flees quickly, rejoice and praise God; but if he is stubborn you must continue steadfastly to resist him, holding the Blood against him, *knowing* that God's remedy always accomplishes just what God says it will accomplish—overcome the enemy. But *mix faith with the Word*

watchfulness is the price of constant victory. "Be vigilant (watch all the time) because your adversary the devil as a roaring lion walketh about, seeking whom he may devour." 1 Peter 5:8.

Our enemy is so set on our destruction that he never sleeps, or neglects to follow after us to destroy us. How sad that we, who have so much at stake, should be less diligent than he. A failure to watch, also gives the devil a place in us or permits him to return. "I say unto all, Watch." We are not safe from his attacks one moment, without the blood of Jesus. As soon as we waken in the morning we should cry for the Blood to be upon us, within us, around us, and between us and all evil and the author of evil. The last thing before we sleep we should, in the same way, cry for the protection of the Blood. Even in the night the true bride of Christ in the Song of Solomon, cries out, "I sleep, but my heart waketh."

Oh, that we could rouse ourselves to a greater intensity in the things of God. We are so halfhearted and yet we must overcome an enemy that is constantly alert and ready to take advantage of all carelessness and neglect. Soldiers are severely dealt with for even a small carelessness or neglect. If we neglect to watch, can God call us good soldiers? Oh, how much we suffer because we fail to watch all the time. "I say unto *all*, Watch." Not one person is excused from watching. We shall never in this life get to a place where the enemy cannot attack us, but God is not willing that we should be overcome even once, *"always* causeth us to triumph in Christ"—not one failure as we obey and trust.

God gives a special promise in Rev. 2:26, 28 to

those who *keep* His works to the *end*. "He that over-cometh and keepeth My works unto the end, to him will I give *power*," and "I will give him the Morning Star," which is Jesus in all His fullness—His life, health, strength, holiness, righteousness, faith, love, meekness, patience—*all* of Jesus. What an incentive to overcome and *keep* all God does in us.

After God has given a healing touch to our bodies let us overcome the devil when he tries to put sickness back upon us. Let us meet him at every point by holding the blood of Jesus on ourselves and against him and *know* that Satan will *surely* flee every time because the Blood is *God's* remedy and *cannot fail.*

CHAPTER 8

GOD'S WILL

Every true child of God desires to be obedient to Him, but sometimes we overlook His expressed will. I believe many fail to do His will as expressed in 1 Thess. 5:16-18. God says in verse 18 that this is His will for everyone in Christ. In verse 16, He bids us "Rejoice evermore." We naturally rejoice when things go well and in times of blessing, but when days are dark; when God does not *seem* to be with us in joy and power; when Satan *seems* to be victorious and we *seem* to be defeated (it only *seems* so); when we are despised, rejected, and our names cast out as evil; when those we have loved and trusted fail us and fail God; when our labor and toil for God *seems* wasted; when we are shut in by evil power and can see no way out; when every earthly hope seems blasted, do we not often mourn at these times? "Evermore" is a broad word that leaves *no time* out, and to do God's will is to rejoice at these times also. Why? It is enough for God's child to know God has commanded it, but God's commands are always intended to do us great good and will always do that if fully obeyed.

The place of joy is the place free from the curse. We read in Job that *all* the sons of God shouted for joy, before the curse came, but a part of that curse was, that there should be sorrow. Paul says "Christ *hath* redeemed us (bought us away) from the curse." Gal. 3:13. Not from a *part* of it, but from *all* of it,

41

and that includes *all* sorrow. Satan brought sorrow to Eve and tries daily to bring sorrow to us, and if we let it rest upon us, we get back under that part of the curse, and suffer. But, if we obey God and rejoice, even though we do not feel like it, Satan and sorrow shall flee away.

We need to be strong and the Word says, "The joy of the Lord is your strength." Neh. 8:10. As we rejoice and praise, even though the heart may be aching, God will make a change and really put joy in the place of sadness.

Rejoicing makes us useful. Satan makes sinners believe that if they become Christians, they will lose all enjoyment. God needs people to prove Satan a liar by letting the well of joy within them flow out in continual rejoicing, so that sinners may know that the well is there. I have talked to infidels who have said, "I can disbelieve your teaching, but your life of joy and contentment must come from God, because others have more material good things than you have and yet have not the joy you have." I have also noticed that careless persons, whom I had failed to interest in the things of God, became interested, at once, when I told them of the joy God had given me. A woman just saved said to some professing Christians—"If you had told me of the joy God would give me, I would have sought Him long ago." But best of all, the Word says that God meets him that rejoiceth.

God is not satisfied to meet us occasionally, but wishes to meet us constantly, and so bids us rejoice continually. One says, "How can I rejoice when all goes wrong?" Ah! the rejoicing is to be in Christ, and not in things, and there is all in Him to make us rejoice. If we would but meditate upon all He is and all He has done, we should have enough to keep us rejoicing through time and eternity, and since neither He nor His work for us ever changes, there need be no change in our rejoicing even though all around us is wrong. God says those who rejoice in Christ are the Israel of God (His peculiarly chosen ones) and also are God's house (and God will take care of His house and keep it in good condition). Oh! let us begin to rejoice and cease not until we meet our Lord and then rejoice through all eternity.

Verse 17 says "Pray without ceasing." We do not cease to think, and God wants a thought of Him to be in *all* our thoughts, and He wishes us to do all we do, even down to eating and drinking, to the glory of God. No matter what we do we are to do it as unto God and not as unto men. If we do this, how constantly we would have to say, "Lord, will this please Thee? How shall I do this to bring glory to Thy name? Enable me in this to honor Thee!" How this would compel us to pray without ceasing, and how different our lives would be! "In *all* thy ways acknowledge Him," can be done only by unceasingly talking to Him about each step we take. To live and move in Him, as the Word tells us to, is to consult Him before we make a single move. Then God would wonderfully keep us,—"Thou wilt keep him . . . whose mind is stayed on Thee."

Verse 18 says—"In *everything* give thanks." Oh! we thank God so much. We thank Him for blessings, answered prayers, for His presence, for joy, peace, healings, etc. True, but do we thank Him for disappointments, hardships, privations, sufferings, losses, crosses, attacks of the enemy, desertions, neglects, mis-representations, etc.? "Everything" takes in all these and all else that can come to a child of God, and God says it is His will that we shall thank Him for them. Why? Because they are great blessings in disguise, and are the instruments that God will use to conform us to the exact image of His Son, if we receive them with thanksgiving. But, if we mourn and repine and beg to be freed from them, God cannot use them to perfect us, and we thus hinder Him from doing what we have asked Him to do—that is, to make us like Jesus. We may finish God's will along other lines, but these parts of God's will shall be ours to continue to do until we meet Him. We may at times be in doubt as to God's will for us along some lines, but He has made this perfectly plain. We may be in places and circumstances where we cannot do some things God would be pleased to have us do, but we can do these things in all places, at all times and under all circumstances, if we set our heart to do them and cry to God for enabling grace. God has a different will for different ones of His children, but this, He says is His will for everyone that belongs to Christ. In some things people hinder us from doing God's will. They hindered even Jesus by their unbelief, but these are personal matters between our soul and God, and none can hinder us. Who of us will set our heart to do God's will in full, along these lines and say from our heart, as did our Blessed Lord, "I delight to do Thy will, O God"?

CHAPTER 9

"ENDURE"

We are told, in 1 Cor. 13:7, that charity (love) endureth all things. James 5:11 says, "We count them happy which endure." Why? Because, "He that shall endure unto the end, the same shall be saved." Matt. 24:13. There is something very solemn in these words, for if those who endure are saved, what about those who do not endure?

What is it to endure? To move steadily on in the way, work, and will of the Lord, even when things are very different from what we wish them to be, is endurance. Paul endured when he said, "None of these things move me." They might buffet him, but could not affect him nor stop his march onward. In James 1:12 we read, "Blessed is the man that endureth temptation." To endure temptation is to move on in full obedience to the Word and to the Spirit and see to it that we do not yield to the temptation, or let our desires reach out to it, or even allow our mind to think on it. As soon as we are conscious of a temptation, we must so yield our whole being to God, His Word, His praise and worship, that there shall be no room in us for the temptation to enter, and none of our members shall yield to it in service or obedience.

We read further in James 1:12 that the man who endureth temptation is blessed, because "When he is tried, he shall receive the crown of life, which the

Lord hath promised to them that love Him." The fourteenth verse of this chapter says that "Every man is tempted, when he is drawn away of his own lust." This word "lust" means strong desire. We may be drawn away from the narrow path that leads to life by our own desires. Jesus said that pathway was so narrow that few find it. Matt. 7:14. Few Christians, comparatively speaking, tempted by their desires, so endure as to keep in that narrow way which means to them fullness of life for spirit, soul and body. God wants us to be so filled with His own life that we shall have power to resist sickness, disease, and pain. God says in Rev. 1:6 that He "hath made us kings" and that we are to *"reign* in life." Rom. 5:17. But it is only those who endure, waver not, fail not when tempted, who really reign and who receive the crown of life, for the Word says it is for those who love God, and the test of love is full obedience.

In 2 Tim. 2:3 we are commanded to "Endure hardness as a good soldier of Jesus Christ." It is so easy to endure when God is blessing and people are pleased, but in connection with this (ninth verse) Paul says that he suffers "as an evil doer, even unto bonds." Did you ever suffer in that way? When you had done your best for God and for people and had walked in His Word, did someone find fault, criticise, judge, and condemn you and represent your work as evil? Did you endure by quietly walking on as though they had praised you? Did someone try to put bonds on you by saying that you must not do the Lord's work in the way you are doing and lay down rules for you to do it their way? Did you then endure by continuing to work as God's Word led you, keeping sweet, gentle, meek, and lowly, with never a word, look or feeling against them? If you were hurt, sad, offended, or willful, or murmured, or grew slack in your work, you did not endure. Did you bear the trouble with long-suffering and joyfulness, like Peter and John, who rejoiced that they were counted worthy to suffer for Christ's sake? Did you work on as Paul did, not being moved in purpose or feelings? That would be enduring. When those for whom you have borne and done the most, forget it all and do you evil in return, do you endure it like Jesus, by never saying a word of defense for yourself and serving them whenever possible as though you did not remember the wrong? That is enduring.

Do you meet scarcity of money, food, clothing, comforts or necessities of life, cheerfully, without talking or even thinking about it, but, like Paul, learn to be abased? Have you ever toiled for God, and seen His work prosper in your hands after you have made great sacrifice for it, only to have someone else, who has stood still and looked on, take all the credit, honor, control and best place in the work you had suffered to build up? Did you smile and care not for the approval of people, because you had the approval of God, and that satisfied you? Did you keep free from all bitterness and rejoice that the work prospered, and did you do all in your power to cause it to prosper even while others received all the credit? That is enduring hardness. In 2 Tim. 2:11 Paul tells us how we can endure, "For if we be dead with Him, we shall also live with Him." See how the thought of endurance is linked with life. But death to our own feelings, desires, choices and comfort must precede the fullness of life. We are also told that we can endure by keeping our eyes on Jesus and not on people—"Endure as seeing Him who is invisible."

Heb. 12:7 speaks of enduring chastening, and in the ninth verse is the assurance that if we endure, we shall "live." Jesus came that we might have life, but to know the fullness of His life we must endure. How do we meet the trials? When God delays answers to prayer, do we continue to believe just as though we saw the answers? Do we carefully and fully meet all the conditions, ask for the thing desired, believe that we receive it when we pray (Mark 11:24), rejoice, thank and praise God as we would if we could see, feel and use the thing for which we prayed? Are we kept from any fear, question, doubt, or wavering? That is enduring.

When God permits people or things to cause us suffering, do we rejoice? When our efforts for Him and His cause seem to fail, are we as full of trust and courage and work as we would be if we were seeing great results? In such a case our endurance would be based on what He has said: "Knowing your labor is not in vain," "In due season ye shall reap," "He that goeth forth and weepeth, bearing precious seed, shall doubtless come again with rejoicing, bringing his sheaves with him." This is enduring. In 1 Peter 2:19 we read of enduring grief, suffering wrongfully. When you are accused of things of which you are not guilty, or are punished for the wrongs of others, or when people separate you from their company and cast out your name as evil, do you endure by rejoicing? Peter refers to Christ as our example. 1 Peter 2:21-23. All Christ's sufferings were for others, for the evil they had done, and for things of which He was falsely accused. Do we endure just as Jesus did with not a word, not a murmur, not a change of purpose or conduct? In Heb. 12:3 we are told to consider how Jesus endured. We do not truly endure unless we meet and pass through hard things just as Jesus did; not murmuring or telling others or talking back; with no change of purpose, work, or attitude toward others.

How *long* must we endure? To the *end*. Matt. 24: 13. How *much* must we endure? *All* things. 1 Cor. 13:7. Not one thing can come to us that is not included in the "all things." *How* must we endure? As Jesus did. Rev. 3:21 says that we are to overcome even as Jesus overcame, and to endure through His strength is to overcome. In Rev. 2:7 we read that the overcomer is to eat of the tree of life, so we see that life is the reward of enduring, fully overcoming. I believe, if we truly endure, fully overcome at all times, Satan will not be able to put disease upon us, because God will so fill us with the more abundant life of the Lord Jesus Christ, that we would be enabled to resist and keep out all disease. Rom. 8:2, 11, 13. Only divine love can enable us to endure, such love to God that we would rather die than fail Him, a love to people that will cover their sins, even a multitude of them. 1 Peter 4:8; Prov. 10:12. If I fail to endure, even once, I need to get down before God and wait upon Him until the "Holy Ghost sheds abroad the love of God in my heart." Charity (love) endureth all things and the proof that I have this love is, that I endure always.

Romans 8:11 But if the Spirit of Him who raised Jesus from the dead dwells in you, He who raised Christ from the dead will also give life to your mortal bodies through His Spirit that dwells in you.

CHAPTER 10

THE POWER OF THE BLOOD OF JESUS CHRIST

God says His people are like sheep in the midst of wolves. So God has given us a wonderful weapon to use, the blood of Jesus. This is our weapon, our shield, our hiding place. We read in Luke 22:20: "Likewise also the cup after supper, saying, This cup is the new testament in My blood, which is shed for you." He had spoken of taking the bread before this. I am so glad He said of the blood that it is "for you." If I were to take anything that belonged to you without your telling me I could do so, that would be presumption; so I am glad Jesus said, "which is shed for you." So long as we are walking in obedience to Him we have a right to that blood every moment. Jesus said, "it is the new testament in my blood." He tried to teach spiritual things by comparing them with things which they could understand, and when He wanted to make them know how sure His covenant is, He used as an illustration the most stable covenant that earth knows anything about. When some tribes and people enter into a covenant they prick the arm, or some part of the body, and put some of the blood on those who make the agreement with them. This means that every drop of their lifeblood should be poured out if necessary to keep that covenant or pledge. So when Jesus says, "This cup is the new testament in My blood," He means every promise in this book, every part of this covenant that He makes with us is to be kept even at the cost of every bit of His lifeblood. Can you doubt a promise sealed like that? Can you be weak in faith when Jesus tells you that all His life and strength shall be poured out before that promise shall fail? Could anything make you more confident than that? The Blood represents the life. The Word says, "The blood is the life." Gen. 9:4. The Blood poured out represents death. His covenant is the blood covenant, and it is the Blood of the everlasting covenant; it is for time and eternity.

The Blood cleanses. The Word tells us that our sins are blotted out by the Blood. "If we confess our sins He is faithful and just to forgive us our sins, and to cleanse us from all unrighteousness." 1 John 1:9. It is blessed to know that all our past sins are gone—blotted out forever; but He goes further than that; He removes those evil desires, cravings and characteristics produced by habitually yielding to the urgings of the selfish nature; but when we fully consecrate all we are and have to Him and have our wills firmly set to obey Him in all things, He causes us to govern our lives by the law of love—that is He puts within us a heart of flesh and the mind that was in Christ Jesus. So many people struggle and strive and fight against lack of love, unbelief, doubt, etc., but they do not get victory. A sister told me that the Lord once opened her eyes to the impatience in her life, and she fought and struggled against it, and she said: "Do you think I improved a bit? No, indeed. But there came a day when I saw that the Blood was to destroy that thing in me, and I trusted the Blood to do it, and very soon I had the victory."

When you see anything in you that produces the transgression, remember that His blood will take that away. Then He says, "Reckon yourselves dead." Count on it; that it is really true. The bearing about in your body the death of the Lord Jesus makes that thing in you really dead and separated from you. He says we are redeemed, not with corruptible things, such as silver and gold, but with the precious blood of Jesus.

We read in the Old Testament that, if we, His children, keep His laws, He will put none of the diseases upon us, which were brought upon the Egyptians, so we see that sickness is the result of the broken law, and this Blood redeems us from sin, and also from sickness, for He bore the curse of the broken law. We must trust the blood of Jesus to deliver us from pain and sickness and disease, for that Blood has bought us away from disease. My prayers seem so poor and worthless, so weak and insignificant. It is blessed to know then that Jesus Christ is seated at the right hand of God making intercession for us. And the Bible says that the Holy Ghost also makes intercession; and also that the Blood cries, or speaks for us.

How often we ask other Christians to pray for us; but oh, how much more precious it is to know that these three are interceding for us; Jesus on the throne; the Holy Ghost in you, His temple, and the Blood. God said to Cain, "Thy brother's blood crieth to Me from the ground." Abel was just a man, but that blood cried to God and He heard it; and Paul says that the blood of Jesus "speaketh better things than that of Abel." If the blood of Abel was sufficient to make God work mightily, what will not the cry of the blood of Jesus Christ do? Surely it speaketh better things than that of Abel.

Then God says that we are made nigh by the Blood.
How often we feel there is a distance between us and
God and we long to get a little nearer. God says the
Blood has brought us nigh. We read that in heaven
the robes of the saints are washed white in the blood
of the Lamb. Those that are cleansed must be washed
from the appetites and desires of the flesh. Jesus said
that we are to "drink His blood." So we drink His
blood to make us clean and to give us life; and we
take it to make us nigh. We may not feel nigh, but
God says the Blood makes us nigh and we must believe it. How blessed it is to get nigh to God in these
awful days! Then the Word says the Blood gives us
access to His face, and through this access we see His
marvelous love and His wonderful willingness to give
us what He has promised.

And the Word says we may come with boldness.
In my missionary work I go into many houses, and
every time I go I ask God to give me favor with
the people and access to their hearts. Without the
help of God, I should many times have great timidity
in going; but there are other times when I do not feel
that way because I have been invited. When we come
blood-covered to God we can come with boldness. He
also says, "with confidence." It is the blood of the
everlasting covenant. Why should we not have confidence? God entered into covenant to redeem us
through Jesus' precious blood; and when Jesus said
on the cross, "It is finished," there was not one iota
left out. If any of you made a contract with another
person and he did not fail to keep his part of it, you
would not think of drawing back. If you would not
draw back, do you think God would? Jesus Christ

has fulfilled every part of the covenant for you and for me and it is finished; this God could not draw back, and best of all, He does not want to.

Then God says this Blood prepares us for every good work. How we try to be ready to do some good work! We read in Heb. 13:20, 21, "Through the blood of the everlasting covenant, make you perfect in every good work." This says, *every good work,* no matter what it is. It is not through self-effort, but it is through the Blood that we are to be perfect in every good work; and when we have trusted the Blood to take away every fleshly effort, and realize that it is God that worketh in us, then God has an instrument that He can use. Oh, that we would trust the Blood more to prepare us for service; how much more would God do!

In Revelation 12:11 we are told that, "They overcame him by the blood of the Lamb and by the word of their testimony." Sin, temptation, sickness, disease, everything that comes from Satan is included in that. The Blood overcame him. When anything is overcome, it has no more power. This book says they overcame him by the blood of the Lamb and by the word of their testimony. Not merely by your word or their word, but by your testimony to what God has done coupled with your faith in the Blood is the overcoming accomplished. No matter in what way the enemy comes, whether in discouragement, temptation, sickness, or any other way, he is overcome by the blood of the Lamb and by the word of our testimony. If ever there was a time when God's children needed to know the power and use of the blood of Jesus, it is now. We are in the last days, and God says in

Therefore brethren, having boldness to
Heb 10:19 enter the Holiest
by the blood of Jesus

THE POWER OF THE BLOOD OF JESUS CHRIST 55

these days there will be seducing spirits. Demons become like angels of light, beautiful, and apparently good. The enemy tries to deceive in every possible way and rages because his time is short. Jesus is coming soon, and God is going to have some that will be ready to meet Him, some that have been made overcomers through the blood of the Lamb. What a wonderful gift Jesus made us when He gave us His precious Blood! Then, there is a text that tells us this Blood gives us access to the very Holy of Holies (Heb. 10:19) where we are shut away from all evil spirits and shut in with God, where we worship and praise and adore Him. It is only the Blood that can shut out the clamor of voices and shut us in with Him.

The Blood witnesses that Jesus Christ has redeemed us from the power of sin, and that we belong to Him, purchased by His blood; that the devil has no claim upon or jurisdiction over us. It is a witness that we are His and that He is ours. That is why we cry continually for the Blood to be upon us. When Satan tries to put any of his work on us we may say, "I have a right to be free from this, for Jesus bought me away from you. You have no claim on me." This is the witness that we belong to Jesus Christ, spirit, soul, and body, for time and for eternity. And God ever works for this precious Blood. When the blood was on the door of the Israelites in Egypt, no evil dared to come through that door. We are safe because of protection of the Blood.

Then, God says that all things are reconciled by the Blood. Col. 1:20; Eph. 2:16. Sometimes we eat food that is not naturally good for us, but if we cry out for the Blood to reconcile it, we know it will not

Having made peace by the Blood

hurt us. Sometimes we meet people who are not of one accord with us, but if we are reconciled to Jesus, and they are reconciled, then we can be reconciled to them through the precious Blood. If, instead of arguing with them, we would cry out for the Blood to reconcile us to them, how much better it would be. I want to give you some instances showing that God does really stand by His promises concerning the Blood.

I was down in Mexico when so many bandits were active, and at one time was in a town when the United States authorities sent us word to get out, that we were in great danger, the red-flaggers were coming. Then the Mexican authorities also sent us word to get out. Nearly all the families went away and they asked me to go, but God did not give me any liberty to go, although the authorities did not promise me any protection. However, I told them I was not looking to them to take care of me, but was trusting God; and, as He was taking care of me, I was just as safe surrounded by those marauders as when alone.

One day I heard a noise and looking out, I saw the Mexican soldiers coming. I never thought of danger, although the road ran very close to my door. I went and stood in the doorway to look in their faces and see what they were like (I tell this to show how God had taken the fear away). I was in a large adobe house all alone with God, and I went to bed and slept sweetly all night. These soldiers were in the town two days and nights, and usually they took the largest house in town (I was in the largest), but they entered every house except mine, and did not come into my house at all.

One day two officers came to the house and stood opposite the door. I saw they wanted something and walked to the door. They said, "Can you tell us where we can get some feed for our horses?" I told them I could not, but they did not come in to see if I was lying to them, as they usually do, but tipped their hats and went away. Now in such time of war we need to cry out for the protection of the Blood. If a mother has a son and she is a Christian, she can put the Blood on the door and claim his salvation and protection. That Blood cries to God and God hears the cry. It is the one thing that will keep you safe in these days of such awful danger.

In a town in Texas there were four persons in an auto; they were struck by a train and three of them were killed, but one girl in that auto was under the protection of the Blood, and she came out without a scratch. In Mexico there are scorpions, and many people die as a result of their sting. One of our missionaries was stung by one of them, and it seemed that he would die or lose his arm, the sting is so poisonous; but God answered prayer, and the missionary lived and did not lose the arm. I was once stung by one of them, but cried out for the Blood to be upon it, and it did not swell nor pain me; the poison could not take hold because of the power of the Blood.

This Blood avails for all things; it is our protection against everything if we will cry for it and trust in it. At one time I walked to a town about six miles distant, as the mules and horses were all away. On my way back I was some distance from any house, when I saw a company of men sitting and drinking muscale (Mexican whiskey), and I saw they were becoming quite drunk with it. I left the path and circled around, but perceiving one of them had seen me and was coming after me as fast as he could, and was rapidly gaining on me at every step; I saw my danger and cried out for the Blood to protect me from this drunken man. Almost immediately his attention was attracted by some little thing along the road and he seemed to forget all about me.

Another time I was coming home from a visit and was not near any house or protection, when I saw a heavy cloud in the distance. The rain comes down in torrents there in Mexico, and it is very bad to be caught in such a storm. I cried out for the Blood and said, "Lord, don't let me get wet." That rain did not touch me; it came near, but did not get to me.

One day I was starting to go into a house, and just as I stepped inside the gate, there was a terrible, ferocious bulldog. I held my umbrella in front of me but he broke it in an instant; then he grabbed me close to the knee, holding my limb between his teeth. I cried for the protection of the Blood, and that dog could not shut his jaws. The people in the house were greatly surprised that I was not torn to pieces.

The mines in Bisbee, Arizona, are very dangerous. One day a man of God was working in one of them when he heard a voice say to him that there was danger there. He saw nothing, but obeyed the voice and got away from the place where he was, and in a few minutes a rock, half the size of a house fell right where the man had been and he would have been killed if he had not known the voice of God and trusted in the Blood.

I went into a house one day and found the whole family down with a fever similar to yellow fever; it is very dangerous. No one would come to help them because they were afraid of it. I felt that I could not leave them that way, so I cried out for the protection of the Blood and stayed with them all that day and night, going from one bed to another waiting on them. I never had a sign of the fever.

Even death has to recede before this precious blood of Jesus. A woman in Douglas had consumption. Her husband was a railroad man and friends telegraphed him that his wife was dying. In their house was a friend who believed in Divine Healing and she sent for me. We had prayer and the woman was better, but the devil came in an onslaught. When I went back my friend said she had a sort of vision and everything in the room was black, except herself and me, and we were like two white specks. She said, "I know death has struck her," and I saw that her face was ashy. I just bent over her and pleaded the power of the blood of Jesus Christ. After a while she drew a long breath, opened her eyes and said: "It is gone." Surely, death had fled before the mighty name and the blood of Jesus. She is a well woman today.

I do not believe we half know the gift Jesus Christ gave us when He gave us this Blood. "He that eateth My flesh, and drinketh My blood, dwelleth in Me." John 6:56. Many precious people are not abiding; they get sidetracked. What is the matter? They are not continually eating His flesh and drinking His blood. It is this precious Blood that enables us to abide. Oh, that we might cry out for it and find shelter under it continually!

CHAPTER 11

Resisting the Devil

"Resist the devil, and he will flee from you." James 4:7. This is a truth that God declares in His Word. Our belief or unbelief in this truth does not affect it in the least, but unbelief keeps us from having the benefit of it. All the evil we have, or that can come to us, is from the devil, directly or indirectly. When he is compelled to flee from us, the evil cannot continue to be fastened upon us. If it is being kept there by the power of the devil, when he flees his power goes with him and the evil loosens and falls from us. The same power that sends the devil away will also cleanse our evil heart, from which Jesus declared so many evils proceed. Matt. 15:19.

Our whole being, spirit, soul and body, has been redeemed—bought away from Satan's power at a great cost, and he no longer has a right to molest any part of us. There is a place where "that wicked one toucheth him not," and that is in our city of refuge, Christ Jesus. God says in Proverbs 18:10 that we may run into His name, which is a strong tower, and be safe. His name represents Himself. The enemy has no right to touch us if we abide there, but he will try to do so. Our protection, deliverance, and safety lie in knowing how to overcome the devil.

God has given us the blood of Jesus and says that it overcomes Satan as we testify to its power, which means that it will rob the devil of his power to harm us. We read in 1 John 5:4, "This is the victory that overcometh ... even our faith." Rev. 12:11 says, "They overcame him (the devil) by the blood of the Lamb and by the word of their testimony." Faith in the blood of Jesus, and in what God has said in His Word, when exercised in testimony against the devil, will always cause him to flee. 1 Peter 5:9 says, we are to be steadfast in resisting the devil. We are never once to think he *can* remain or keep evil upon us, because God has said that if we resist him he *will* flee, and God's Word *cannot* fail. So there is only one thing to see to, and that is to resist the devil until he goes, be the time long or short. We should keep covered and protected by the Blood constantly by asking God to cover us with it, and believing that He does so *now,* when we ask.

When Satan attacks us in spirit, soul or body, we must quickly meet him with the powerful blood of Jesus and add to it our "word of testimony," which means God's declaration through us that the Blood does overcome Satan. This is resisting the devil and we have God's sure Word that when we resist him he will flee.

We were born under the control of the devil, and we are to resist his dominion over us by refusing to obey him, or let any of our members serve him.

We are to resist the sins, appetites, passions, and evil desires which he has put upon us, by asking God to put the blood of Jesus against the devil and the evil within, and then believe that God does put the Blood there when we ask Him to do so, and that it does what God says it will do—overcomes the devil and destroys his work.

We are to overcome all fear, depression, unbelief, wavering and halfheartedness in the same way.

We are to overcome disease, pain, sickness, and weakness. We must have hands laid on us, as God has commanded, and believe that God's healing power enters our body and heals us. Then, we must ask God to put the Blood against the devil, and upon all the symptoms of disease or infirmity, believe, because God says it does, that the blood of Jesus *now* overcomes them, and assert upon God's unfailing Word—"The blood of Jesus overcomes the devil and all he has done within me."

You have used the Blood and the word of your testimony; your faith must now be added to these. You must truly believe that Satan and his work *are now* overcome, and that they do flee, even though you see and feel no change. "Faith is the evidence of things *not* seen." To believe only what you see and feel is not faith at all—that is knowledge. Faith never deals with anything but the *unseen* and the *unfelt*. You are to call the "things which be *not* as though they were." Rom. 4:17. Believe that the devil and the disease have gone, that healing and soundness do *now* take their place and that you are well. This faith compels the exchange because faith overcomes. God always gives everybody just what they believe for (Matt. 9:29), and faith, the Blood and the testimony drive out the evil things.

Many of God's children have learned to come to Him and receive His healing touch, but many have not learned how to resist the devil when he tries to put sickness upon them. God is so kind and loving that He delights to heal all sickness, but His highest will for us is that we shall be kept free from sickness by His almighty power.

1 Peter 4:12 says your faith will be tried. This trial consists of seeing and feeling the old symptoms still, but true faith believes God's Word and refuses to believe any symptoms. Sometimes faith is tried by a return of old symptoms, after our having been healed and freed from them. Sometimes the pain and disease come back just as they were before the healing. The Blood, the testimony, and faith must again be used. Declare that God *has* healed and that Satan cannot put the disease back because you still resist him; steadfast in faith, without doubt, fear, or wavering. As you thus stand, Satan and all symptoms will indeed flee as God has said they will. The Bible tells us that Satan will say, "I will go back to the place from whence I came out," but if the Blood and faith are there, he has to leave.

As long as we are in Satan's territory—this world—he will try to attack us, and for this reason we should constantly ask God to cover us and surround us with the blood of Jesus, believe He does so, and also believe that Satan cannot harm us because of the Blood. In Luke 10:19 Jesus says, "I give you power . . . over all the power of the enemy," and this power is in the blood of Jesus, and by faith in His blood, to which we testify. The Blood and the Word are all-powerful but it takes true faith to set this never-failing power to working. Use the Blood and the Word against Satan wherever he attacks you in spirit, soul, or body and know that they take from Satan all power to put anything on you or to keep anything on you, because God, who cannot lie, says these things overcome the devil every time.

Your own mouth can hasten the victory greatly. God says in Mark 11:23, you shall have what you say if you do not doubt. Say, "I refuse to have this sickness," no matter how much Satan tries to make you feel or see it. Eph. 4:27 says, "Neither *give* place to the devil." God means here that the devil cannot get a place to put sins, pain, or disease upon you if you resist him all the time by the Blood, the word of your testimony and faith. We must always watch. If we thus refuse Satan a place in us or on us, he cannot *take* a place for himself.

Never say, "I have pain, disease, doubt, or other evil." Say, "I will not have it. I will not let Satan put it on me. I refuse to accept it or recognize it or own it." Continue to say, "I am delivered, no matter how I feel or look." Praise hastens victory. Believe the thing is *done*, praise and rejoice, not because it is going to be done, but because it is done, even though you cannot see it nor feel it. The Bible says, "Thou meetest him that rejoiceth" (Isa. 64:5), and God will meet you by making real in your experience the things that you rejoice in by faith.

The Word tells us that the Blood overcomes Satan and that he *does* flee. Plant your feet upon these truths, *use* the remedy and never relax until victory comes. It must come because God has said it will. It is far easier to drive Satan back when he first attacks us than after he has a hold upon us. Besides that, his touch is defiling. So, instead of letting him afflict us and then seeking deliverance, let us see that he does not get a place in or upon us. I believe that many people open

the door and permit Satan to enter by thinking "I have"
—whatever he may be trying to put upon them—yielding to it and ceasing to refuse and to resist.

I arose one morning and found that I could not stand
—I reeled like a drunkard. I said, "This is of you,
Satan; I *hold* the Blood against you, and declare on
God's Word that it does now overcome you, and that
you do *now* flee." The enemy was stubborn, but I continued to believe and repeat what I said until every
trace of the trouble was gone. I then did a full day's
hard work, and have had no return of the evil. Many
times I have awakened feeling very sick all over. I
am sure that if I had yielded I would have been in bed
unable to do anything, but as I resisted, Satan and all
his symptoms went, and I did hard work all day until
late at night and went to bed well.

A lady resisted smallpox for herself and family. One
of them broke out with it, but she seated herself by the
bed and told God she would not cease to resist until the
disease went. Every bit of the disease disappeared, and
no one else took it. She resisted steadfastly even when
God did not seem to hear, and found Him faithful who
had promised.

I have found that as I continually meet Satan with
the Blood, and never release until he flees, the Blood
works quickly and more powerfully. I am sure it will
do the same for you, dear reader, if you will set to
your seal that God is true, that the Blood is infallible,
and His promises sure.

Gal. 6:9 says, "Be not weary . . . for in due season
we *shall* reap if we faint not." God's time is *now*, and,
if you are all right, you should have immediate victory;
but you must begin with a fixed purpose never to stop

until you have full victory. Jesus won it for you on the cross, and all you have to do is to hold fast without a doubt, or waver, or weakening until it is felt and seen. God the *Almighty One* says you *shall* reap if you do not faint—which means ceasing to believe and to resist, or becoming less earnest and persistent. The more stubborn Satan is, the more earnest and persistent you must be.

Gal 6:9
Reap if you do not
faint.

CHAPTER 12

WHATSOEVER WE ASK

"The effectual, fervent prayer of a righteous man availeth *much*." James 5:16. God *says* prayer avails *much* and He also gives us the record of great things caused by prayer. Joshua prayed and the sun stood still. Nineveh prayed and God reversed His death sentence upon them. Hezekiah prayed and God moved the time of his death forward fifteen years. Samson prayed and God restored his lost power. Daniel prayed and God shut the lions' mouths. Elisha, Paul and Peter prayed and dead people came to life. Elijah prayed and no rain fell for three and a half years, and he prayed again and rain came. God foresaw that people would say that God had given Elijah special prayer privileges because he was a prophet, and therefore He tells us that he was just a man of like passions as ourselves. Then why cannot we get answers to our prayers? One says, "I do." But do you get answers to *all* your prayers?

Listen! God says, "*Whatsoever*" we ask we receive. Whatsoever means *any* thing—*every* thing—*all* things. Do you always get whatsoever you ask? God tells us in several places in the Bible that this is His will for us, but there are conditions. Failure to get answers to prayer is because the conditions are not met. We cannot tease or coax God into answering prayer when conditions are not met, but He delights to answer when they are met.

1 John 3:22 says God will answer all prayer if we will obey Him and please Him. To keep His commandments is to obey *all* the New Testament. To please Him is to cease to try to please ourselves, or people, and to do all we do with the thought, effort and desire to please God and Him only. Jesus makes this clear in John 15:7, "If ye *abide* in me and My words abide in you, ye shall ask *what ye will* and it *shall* be done." In 1 John 2:6 we are told that abiding in Him means living as Jesus lived. 1 John 3:24 says if we obey Him, we abide in Him. 1 John 4:16 says if we *dwell* in love (love God and *everybody all* the time) we abide in Him. John 6:56 says to abide in Him is to eat His flesh and drink His blood.

As we sum up these tests we see that to abide in Christ is to put away all sin, disobedience, self, and our own way, and be *one* with Christ. To what extent? "As Thou Father art in Me, and I in Thee." John 17:21. To be, as Paul said, "I am crucified (separated completely from myself) ... Christ liveth in me." Gal. 2:20. "He that is joined unto the Lord is one Spirit." 1 Cor. 6:17. Have you noticed the joinings in a piano case? It is difficult to tell where one piece ends and another begins. God wants us so to sink into Christ that those who meet us cannot tell where the human ends and the divine begins.

To yoke with Him means to do not one thing apart from Him and to do all that He does even as two oxen yoked together have to move and stop together and go the same way. Some have thought that asking in Jesus' name means to use the name of Jesus in the prayer. The meaning is far deeper. It means to "Put on the Lord Jesus" by thinking, speaking, acting, and living just as Jesus would if He were in your place. This is to abide in Him and ask what ye will and get it.

How did He walk? "I do *always* those things that please Him (the Father)." John 8:29. "I never seek to please Myself. I seek not My glory or honor but the honor of Him that sent Me. I do not desire honor but 'make Myself' of *no* reputation."

He took no credit for the works He did but said, "The Father that dwelleth in Me, He doeth the works." John 14:10. He even told some not to tell of the works He did for them. He never murmured against God or people who mistreated Him. He said, "I judge *no man*." He never criticized, found fault, or told others of the faults of people. He took the lowest place—foot washing. He was the Son of God, but called Himself the Son of man—the lowest place. He did His Father's will when it made Him to be "despised and rejected of men"—when it brought the sufferings of Gethsemane and Calvary upon Him and caused God to forsake Him. It was this life of full, constant obedience, with no self-seeking or self-saving, that pleased the Father and this is the life we must live to abide in Him, so that we may realize the promise of, "Ask what ye will and it *shall* be done."

We must abide in love as He did. When the disciples were self-seeking and striving, He did not chide them but just set them an example. The city that treated Him the worst was the one He wept over and desired to gather under His wings. The man who denied Him was the one He honored by name in His call to the disciples to meet Him. The man that had sold Him was one to whom He was most gracious at the Last Supper. The men who nailed Him to the cross were the ones for whom He uttered His last intercessory prayer. To eat His flesh and drink His blood is to take His life into us and to reproduce it—to walk in Him. To live thus is to *be* in His name.

John 14:13 says we are to ask in Jesus' name that the Father may be glorified. Not a prayer is to be made with a selfish motive. You cannot find one prayer of Jesus' that had only good for Himself as its object—always it was for the glory of the Father and for the extension of the kingdom. To ask in His name is to see to it that what we ask is *always* asked in order that we may better glorify God and extend His kingdom—"Seek first the kingdom." In Mark 11:24 we have the "Whatsoever" of prayer limited by "desire." What you do not earnestly desire is not real prayer. "Prayer must express the soul's sincere desire." The things of God have cost Jesus so much that God gives them only to those who truly desire them— "Those who hunger and thirst shall be filled."

In Matt. 21:22 the "Whatsoever" is limited by faith. "Whatsoever ye shall ask in prayer, believing, ye shall receive." Prayer without faith is useless. "He that cometh to God *must* believe." Heb. 11:6. James 1:6, 7 says that if we waver (doubt at times) we shall not receive *anything*. A condition of answered prayer is humility. The publican, who thought so little of himself that he could not look up, got his request. The Pharisee who remembered the good works that he had done, got nothing. Another condition is to get into *your* closet—not the closet of a house—your closet— into your spirit. Shut the door by putting away all thoughts of yourself, people and things, and see and recognize God only. Prayer prayed for others to hear

is not the closet prayer the Father promises to hear
—the door is not shut on you and God alone.

Jesus gave three patterns of prayer. Luke 11:2-4
shows how to pray for yourself. "Our Father" means
to be sure you are born again so that God *is* your Father, and that you are so in love with all His children
and so unselfish that you desire for them all that you
ask for yourself. Worship God by calling Him holy,
desire His kingdom and will, more than the supply of
your own needs and show it by asking for them first.
The request is not to be for a supply to lay up, but
just for the day's need. We must not forget that there
might be, even though forgotten by us, some sin in
the way; and also we must be sure to forgive everyone just in the way we desire God to forgive us.
Matt. 6:12. There must be the purpose in the heart
to keep away from all evil and to resist all temptation.

In Luke 11:5-8 Jesus tells how to pray for the un-
saved. Jesus is *your* Friend, but the friend who comes
to you does not know Him. First feel and confess your
own inability—"I have *nothing*." Let me have three
loaves—Jesus for the spirit, Jesus for the soul, and
Jesus for the body. Jesus declares if you are impor-
tunate, He will open the door that your friend may
have shut by sin, unbelief, and hardness of heart.
Webster's dictionary says that importunity sometimes
means "Coming or asking at an inconvenient or trou-
blesome time," and that may be one aspect of the
meaning here. It is midnight, the door is shut and He
is having close fellowship and communion with the
children—the saved ones. God is not likely to save a
sinner if we ask in an easy way that costs us nothing,
but if we lose sleep, rest, comfort, and ease, and

choose to intercede for the sinner rather than to seek our own enjoyment in the communion, fellowship and blessings of God, "He *will* rise and give him as many as he needeth." *You* will get the closed door open.

Luke 18:2-8 tells us how to pray against Satan, who is our adversary. 1 Peter 5:8. The widow made no request except for vengeance on her adversary. God has promised to bruise Satan under our feet. As God's true elect see the havoc Satan is making daily, hourly, they will cry for God to interfere and really do as He has promised—put Satan down and enable God's children to use the power God has given them over *all* the power of the enemy so that they shall truly tread upon him. God declares He will avenge His own elect who prove they are the elect by their continued crying against the enemy, even at night when others are thinking of self and rest.

Verse 8 shows that the cause of God's having to bear long with them is their unbelief. God has told them that He *has* given them power over *all* the power of the enemy, and told them to give him no place, and that if they resist him, he will flee, but they have not fully believed this. Then Jesus tells us in Mark 11:24 that if we believe we receive, *when we pray* we shall have it. God has given all these conditions, and if we would see *all* our prayers answered, we must not fail on one of them. It is not easy to meet them, but God calls us to it, and His grace can enable us to do it. The joy of getting all our prayers answered is sufficient to cause us to press on until we attain to it. Let us stir ourselves up to meet every condition and truly get "Whatsoever we ask."

CHAPTER 13

Head Faith and Heart Faith

"With the heart man believeth unto righteousness." We have narrowed the word righteousness down to mean only the right condition of the soul. The true meaning of the word is, being right, and it includes spirit, soul and body. When man fell, his whole being suffered through it. God provided a full salvation for the whole man and did all that was necessary to secure this redemption. We can get it by faith.

There is a head faith and a heart faith. The head faith brings us nothing. The heart faith brings us everything that Jesus secured for us, which is perfect rightness in spirit, soul and body. Most people believe with the head only, and so do not get what God has promised. The head sees, understands, and counts things true, but only the heart can appropriate or lay hold of and cling to things that are "Freely given to us of God." 1 Cor. 2:12. The head looks at the surroundings, difficulties and hindrances. The heart looks at the thing desired and the promise of God and refuses to see the hindrances. It is the heart faith that "laughs at impossibilities, and cries, 'It *shall* be done.'" Head faith is strong when things are favorable, but the heart faith is just as strong when all things are against it, because it rests on the Almighty God who rules over persons, powers and things.

Head faith grows weak and fails when the answer

faith resting on my sense or my heart revelation?

is delayed. Heart faith says, "I received when I prayed and the answer is as much mine *now* as it will be when I have it manifested." Head faith says, "Be careful not to profess until you can see, for by so doing you may bring reproach on the cause." Heart faith says, "The thing I am asking is sure to appear soon and confirm my profession and I shall honor His cause because God *always* rewards faith." Head faith says, "There might be a failure." Heart faith says, "Because of God's promise and His oath to keep His promise, it is impossible for failure to come." Head faith says, "I trusted until I saw everything getting worse." Heart faith says, "Though He slay me *yet* will I trust in Him" (Job 13:15), and "I shall yet praise Him for the help of His countenance." Psalm 42:5.

The head reasons about things. God says, "Casting down reasonings (marginal, of imaginations) and every high thing that exalteth itself against the knowledge of God." 2 Cor. 10:5. The heart lays hold of things that are beyond *all* reason; holds fast and expects God to do things that are impossible—contrary to reason. The head investigates as to how God is working, and as to the progress and results. The heart clings to His Word, even when there is nothing in evidence. The head says, "I shall know I have my petition when my senses give evidence that it is in my possession—when I can see it, feel it or otherwise experience it." The heart says, "I *know* I have it *now,* because I have met the conditions and have taken it." It is the heart that stands still and *sees* what, to others, is invisible. It is the heart faith of which Paul is speaking when he says it is "the evidence of things *not* seen."

Head faith gives up easily, but the heart faith is that of Jacob that cries, "I *will* not let Thee go, except Thou bless me." Gen. 32:26. It was heart faith that caused the Syrophenician woman (Matt. 15:22-28) to hold on to Jesus when "He answered her not a word," and not to leave when the disciples wanted Him to send her away. It was heart faith that would not be discouraged, even when Jesus told her that He was not sent to her, because she was not an Israelite and that it was not right to give "the children's bread" to her. Heart faith, when all else has failed, will do what she did—fall down at Jesus' feet in humility and worship until He says, "Be it unto thee even as thou wilt." Jesus will always say that to heart faith when we are seeking anything that God has promised in His Word. It is only to heart faith that He says, "As thou hast believed, so be it done unto thee." Matt. 8:13. Head faith gets discouraged easily, but it is of heart faith that the Bible says, "This is the victory that overcometh the world, even our faith." 1 John 5:4. Jesus said that Satan is the prince of this world. If faith overcomes the world, it must overcome its prince, so the above includes all our spiritual enemies.

If you have been believing for something and have not yet had it in evidence, see if your faith has not been head faith, which is dependent upon seeing, feeling and experiencing before it can rejoice in the answer. See if you have not been reasoning and have not been affected by obstacles in the way. Perhaps you have the head faith that says, "It will be done sometime," instead of the heart faith that says, "It *was* done when I prayed." Oh, exercise the heart faith that deals with the unseen and counts things that be *not*, as though they *were,* and then you will overcome all obstacles, even the devil himself, by that faith which overcomes the world.

The Bible says that God looketh on the heart. He will not see or regard your head faith. He is not looking at your head, so it will not matter how much head faith you have, but He will see heart faith, even when it is as small as a grain of mustard seed, and He will *never* fail to say to that faith, "According to your faith be it unto you." Matt. 9:29. You must remember, however, that it is the heart faith that worketh "by love." If there is in your heart the least bit of dislike for or criticism of even the most trying person, this heart faith cannot work because it worketh *only* by love. The Bible says, "If our heart condemn us not, *then* have we confidence toward God." 1 John 3:21. Many of God's children do not *feel* condemned by things that God's Word condemns. If there is any person I will not forgive and truly love, if I am not willing to obey God fully, if there is pride, selfishness, or willfulness in my heart, these things condemn me before God and hinder my heart faith. It is only when we are abiding in Christ that there is "no condemnation" and we have "confidence (faith) toward God." God says we abide in Christ *only* as we walk, as *He* walked. 1 John 2:6.

Examine your faith and if you have been exercising head faith, exchange it quickly for the heart faith that will bring to you all that God has promised in His precious Word.

CHAPTER 14

THE FAITH THAT TAKES

God has been keeping the word *"take"* before me. It has been estimated that the Bible contains thirty-two thousand promises. God Himself planned and made all the promises. Jesus came and purchased them. At the very close of the Bible we find the word *"take."* Rev. 22:17. God gave us Jesus, all that He is, all that He has, and all that He has done. Also He "hath given unto us all things that pertain unto life and godliness." 2 Pet. 1:3. There is in Jesus all that we can need, for spirit, soul and body, and if we have all that pertains to life and godliness, we also have all we can need for all temporal things. This promise is in the past tense, "hath given"; God gave, hath given and now He entreats us to *take* what He has already given. The Greek word in Mark 11:24, which is translated receive, is a word that means "take with much force, seize with a grip that will not be shaken off."

God laments that "none stirreth up himself to take hold on" God. Isa. 64:7. Every promise of God is a part of His covenant, and it takes real stirring up to put away halfheartedness, doubts, waverings, and unbelief, and to take the things which God has given us. How do we take them? Jesus said, "What things soever ye desire, when ye pray, believe that ye receive (take) them, and ye shall have them." Mark 11:24. The only limit here is a real earnest desire for the things for which we ask. The things of God are so

77

precious, He will not give them to those who do not greatly desire them. It is those who hunger and thirst who are filled. "He *shall* have them"; not hope to have them, but *shall* have them. In 1 John 5:14, 15 we read, "We know that we *have* the petitions that we desired of Him." "Hold that fast which thou hast." Rev. 3:11.

✳ The devil is busy trying to take from us what we take from God, and so God bids us hold fast. Jesus gave Peter power to walk on the water, but the devil took it from him by getting him to fix his attention on the wind (representing things we feel), and on the waves (representing things we see). Peter had the power and used it, but one doubt made him lose it. If we are cleansed, obedient, and separated from all feelings, self, and the world, we can meet the conditions of a promise, ask for what we desire, and take it, by believing that God gives it now. You must then say, "I have it, it is now mine," and then you must keep your eyes on Jesus, refuse to see or feel things that look contrary and wait before God until He lets you see the thing which you have taken from Him by faith. The Bible tells us that God works while we wait, and we are waiting on God only when all our thoughts, attention, and mind, are fixed on Him, and we put away quickly every thought which the devil thrusts upon us. Many take things from God and at once get absorbed in other things, and lose all. Instead of this, wait, praying, thanking, and worshiping until God lets you see. Know that He is working because He says that He works while you wait and He cannot lie, "Said I not unto thee, that, if thou wouldest believe, thou shouldest see?" John 11:40.

Our faith rests only upon His faithfulness who says, "I will not leave thee until I have done that which I have spoken to thee of." Gen. 28:15. Very simple and plain is our part in the obtaining of God's promised blessings, and this laying hold by faith is much easier of accomplishment than most of us are willing to believe. Our part is simply to reckon our prayers as answered, solely on the assurance of the Word of God, and God's part is to make faith's reckonings real. This is by no means a question of feeling our faith, but of acting our faith. After all, we always find ourselves acting upon what we really believe. It is not necessary to feel some particular emotion in our hearts, but to act as though we believed what we profess to believe. God would have us believe His word without any confirmation. It is His part to confirm it with signs following.

Romans 4:17

CHAPTER 15

THINGS THAT BE NOT

Perhaps there is nothing spoken of in the Bible which is quite so hard for most Christians to do as to call "those things which be not as though they were." Many honest people think they would be lying if they did this, and so fear to do it. But consider a moment; the Bible tells us that God cannot lie, and God calls the things that be not as though they were. He speaks of Jesus as "the Lamb slain from the foundation of the world." Rev. 13:8. Jesus did not hang on the cross until thousands of years afterwards. God says that we were chosen in Christ from the foundation of the world, and we were not yet born. God said to Abraham, "I *have* made thee a father of many nations," when he had not even one child. God's greatest desire for His children is that they be like Him in all things. He says that Abraham was made "like unto Him (see margin) whom he believed, even God who quickeneth the dead and calleth those things which be not as though they were." Rom. 4:17. Abraham was made like unto God in this thing, and He tells us to follow in the footsteps of Abraham.

Because God does this and tells us to do it, it is impossible for it to be wrong in the least degree. Sin is disobeying God, and holiness is simply obeying and pleasing God in all things, at all times. God is holy and His will is holy, and when Christ dwells within us, He works through us His own obedience and holiness. One part of God's will is that we shall call those things which be not as though they were. This attitude honors God, because we are believing His Word without outward evidence and thus we please Him; it also puts us in an attitude of faith to receive great things from God. God offers us many wonderful things and tells us to take them. "Whatsoever things ye desire, when ye pray, believe that ye receive (take) them and ye shall have them." Faith is the hand with which we take from God. When we have met all the conditions and taken what God is offering us, we must believe that we *have* that thing. Many things for which we believe can be manifested in a moment, and we should believe for them to come into evidence at once. Other things, from their nature require time, but whether the thing we have prayed for requires time or not, we are to believe that we *receive* it *when* we *pray* for it.

All that we need for spirit, soul, and body is in Jesus. When by faith coming into close contact with Him, we believe His promise and take what we ask for, it is then done according to His word, even though it is not yet realized by our senses. "He that believeth on the Son of God *hath* the witness in himself." 1 John 5:10. Now if we recognize, by faith, that we *have* the thing we have taken, though it is unseen and unfelt, we will praise Him for it, and He will bring it into evidence. Just as He made the moon and stars to appear, He is still the Creator and will create in us and for us whatever He has promised as we meet the conditions, ask, take it, and call it as though it were. Do you need deliverance from unholy tempers and diseases? God says, "Yield yourselves unto God as those that are alive from the dead, and your members as instruments of righteousness unto God." Rom. 6:13. As we thus yield ourselves to God, as having died with Christ, and as having risen with Him, we experience Christ's righteousness dwelling within. Do we need deliverance from pain? Believe that you *are* delivered, even before the pain is removed. Do you need healing from Jesus the great Physician? Believe that you are healed through His Word of promise, even though for a time the disease seems to develop and grow worse. Do you need His strength? Believe that you have it in spite of your seeming weakness. These things are already yours in Christ, and as you take them by faith, you will know, on His Word, that you have them. Recognize their presence while they seem not to be and the great Creator will cause them to be. Often we have opposing forces in us that hinder God from manifesting that for which we are believing. For instance, such things as doubts, fears, unbelief, questionings, murmurings, criticisms, the desiring to see and feel instead of being willing to stand on God's Word alone, may obstruct the manifestation of God's power. Sometimes there is real sin—a lack of love in us or an unforgiving spirit, or bitterness—these will delay the manifestation of what we are seeking to take from God. Let us call the things that be not as though they were, and, if they do not at once appear, let us get rid of whatever is contrary to God's will. Then the unseen things will appear so that you will see, feel and enjoy them. Oh, God is so faithful to fulfill all His promises when we really take Him at His Word.

CHAPTER 16

FAITH AND LOVE

Faith is the hand that takes things from God. All that Jesus purchased can be had by faith. Salvation, healing, the fullness of the Spirit, the fruit, gifts, and graces of the Spirit, victory over sin, the flesh, the world, the devil, evil spirits, and all the powers of darkness may be had by faith, but it must be the "faith which worketh by love." Gal. 5:6.

The Bible says devils believe so intensely that they tremble, but their faith brings no results because they have no love, and God says it is the faith that worketh by love which avails.

Since we must have a faith that works, and which works by love, it will be well for us to see how that sort of faith works.

We are told that "Love covereth *all* sins." Prov. 10:12. 1 Peter 4:8 says "Charity (love) shall cover the multitude of sins." Put the two texts together and we have—love will cover *all* sins even when there is a *multitude* of them. Who can tell how many there are in a multitude? "Multitude" is a word generally used to denote more than you can name. Think of it—real, genuine love will cover, hide, put out of sight more sins than you can name.

Love covers *sins*. Sin is the worst thing in the universe. So God says real love will cover the meanest, most trying, evil thing that *can* come to you, and will keep on covering until all of the great multitude of mean things is covered—hid so you cannot see them and so others cannot see them.

1 Cor. 13:7, in our King James Bible, reads—"Charity beareth all things," but other translators have it—"Love covers all things with silence." So God says love not only hides the evil in others, but refuses even to speak of it.

Then, if we tell of the evil someone has done, criticize, judge, condemn, or murmur against anyone, no matter who he is or what he has done, we are proving that we have not love, because "Love covers with silence." However, this covering of and being silent concerning sins is only as to the sins of others. God says of our own sins that if we cover them we shall not prosper, but that we must forsake and confess them. Prov. 28:13. We are not to love ourselves, but are to love others and to cover their sins. But, do we not often reverse God's order by covering our own sins and exposing the sins of others? We prove that we love the wrong person. It was after Job said, "I *abhor* myself," that God delivered him.

In 1 Cor. 13:4, we are told that love works by being kind even under long continued suffering—real, deep suffering brought upon us by someone else. Love will be very kind to that person.

Love "envieth not." Love does not desire the position, honor, power, benefits, favor, esteem, or blessings that others have, but is glad to see other people enjoy blessings and would rather help them to get more than take from them anything they have.

Love "is not puffed up." Love does not think, "I know how things ought to be done—my opinions and advice are better than the opinions and advice of others —I live better, am used of God more, know more than that other one." The saints are commanded to esteem others better than themselves (Phil. 2:3), and in the next verse to "look not on their own things"—to see what they are, have, and can get,—but to look on the things of others to see the good that they have and do and to see how much they can help the others to get. That is, they unselfishly keep so busy helping someone else that they forget themselves and their own attainments. Phil. 2:4. "In honor preferring one another." Rom. 12:10. One having love is glad to let another have the honor which he could have had.

Love "seeketh not her own." 1 Cor. 13:5. How many of us, when we have a real right to a place, time, honor, benefit or possession, refuse to strive for it, refuse even to seek to keep it, but cheerfully, gladly let another have it?

The above verse also says of love that it "is not provoked." The word easily, in the best Bibles, is in italics, showing that it was not in the original. We have another text which says, "Great peace have they which love Thy law and *nothing* shall offend them." Psalm 119:165. Then if I am offended, no matter how much cause I have to be offended, the matter with me is that I have not the love which nothing will offend.

Love "thinketh no evil." Love has covered *all* evil with silence—will not speak of it—and now goes deeper yet and refuses to *think* on it, but instead will think on things true, lovely, of good report, etc. Phil. 4:8.

Love "endureth all things." 1 Cor. 13:7. To endure is to go through a thing just as though it had not occurred—to be not in the least affected by it. How many of us can and *do* go through *all* trying, hurtful, evil things that are on every side as sweetly, calmly, silently, lovingly, and uncomplainingly as if they all were just as we would like them to be! That is to endure.

These are a few of the ways in which love works. How many of us can say, with our hearts open to the eye of God, "I have the faith that works this way"? God says this is the kind of faith that will avail, and He will not change. Had we not better change?

Think of the marvelous and blessed things without number which God has prepared for us and which we can have for the faith that works by love. Can we afford to do without them? We can easily love good people. It is only bad, trying people that it is hard for us to love. Shall we let some disagreeable, bad people keep us from the glorious things of God? Shall we let our bodies be sick, shall we fail to get the fullness of the Spirit, with His fruit, gifts and graces? Shall we be short of power to overcome *all* evil and fail to get our prayers answered, just because of people who do wrong? Above all, just because we would not see to it that our faith worked by love, shall we be content to have a low place through all eternity, when we might have been full overcomers and might have sat down by Jesus on the throne? God says we are no better than a sinner if we love only the kind and good. See how Jesus loved. He wept over Jerusalem, which persecuted Him more than any other city. He gave Judas, who had just sold Him, what in that country is the token of greatest honor—bread dipped in the sop and given with His own fingers. See how He honored Peter, who above all the other disciples, had denied Him, by having the angel send the message "Tell His disciples and *Peter*." One says, I can love if they cease from evil. Judas had not ceased when Jesus honored him, and we had not ceased from sin when He died for us. He prayed for forgiveness for His murderers while they mocked Him.

I am sure, if we will be really honest and measure ourselves by God's tests of genuine love, we shall see why we have failed to get the many things we need from God. We shall be compelled to admit that our love has not been the genuine article that the Holy Ghost sheds abroad in hearts. Let's cry out for the genuine. We cannot help the past—it is gone. We can help the future. We can secure all that God so graciously offers us in His Word, if we will see to it that our faith works by a love that will measure up to God's tests. "*All* things are possible to him that believeth," but he must believe with a faith that worketh by love, and the test of love Godward is—"If a man love Me he will keep My words." John 14:23. "This is the love of God that we keep His commandments. The test of love manward is to cover *all* sins, refuse to speak, or even think of them, and treat the offending person as if he had never done wrong.

God says, "Follow after love." Let's never cease to follow after love until we have so much of it that we can measure up to each of God's tests of true love and are able to walk in love and to love in *deed*. That means, if we truly desire this love that will cause our faith to bring answers to our prayers, we must ask God to have the Holy Spirit shed abroad this divine love in our hearts, as He has promised in Rom. 5:5, and then act love in looks, words, tone of voice, hearty greetings, etc., to those present, and by loving letters to those absent, and ever seek to do the loving deed.

CHAPTER 17

Does Your Faith Grow?

Paul said that the faith of the Thessalonians grew *exceedingly.* 2 Thess. 1:3. Growth is caused by proper food given at regular intervals, and by exercise. A careful mother gives her baby good food frequently. If a child does not grow, attention is at once given to its food. Satan in these days is trying to make God's children look at their own faith—how much they have and how little, and is getting them to worry because they have so little faith. That will not remedy the wrong. The remedy is good food, given regularly and abundantly. God says "Faith cometh by hearing ... the Word of God." Do not waste time by gazing at your small or weak faith but feed it and it will become strong. Give it the rich, nourishing food of the Word of God regularly and abundantly. God's Word, unlike any other food, will not produce a bad effect by being taken in large quantities. God tells you to let it dwell in you richly—in great abundance.

Faith never acts by itself, but confides in someone or in something. God says He has given to every man a measure of faith, and yet how much more faith we see in some people than in others, because they rest their faith on the right object. If we rest our faith on things or people that fail us again and again, our faith becomes weak. God and His Word never fail, never change and never disappoint. As we believe Him and what He has said, and are careful to meet all the conditions He has given, we shall receive just what He has said we should receive; and thus our faith will grow and be made strong. Faith that rests on what we see or feel or experience will not grow strong, or even continue to live. Heb. 11:1 tells us that faith deals with the unseen, and Jesus told Thomas He would bless those who would dare to believe, although they had not seen, and He meant also those who had not felt, or had any evidence except God's Word.

Psa. 91:4 says that God's truth (His Word) is a shield. Eph. 6:16 says that the shield of faith will quench all Satan's fiery darts, and this is faith in God's Word as it is held between you and Satan. In Rev. 12:11 we read, "They overcame him (Satan) by the blood of the Lamb, and by the word of their testimony," which means the Word of God used in testimony against Satan. Jesus used the Word of God against Satan in His wilderness temptation, and we are told that Satan thereupon left Him for a season, —overcome by the Word of God used against him by the Lord Jesus. Eph. 6:16 says we are to *take* this shield of faith and to hold it up between us and all of Satan's attacks, and that thus his fiery darts will be quenched and be powerless to hurt us.

Faith is not only defensive but is also offensive. We are to "Fight the good fight of faith," and the weapon used is the sword of the Spirit, the Word of God. As faith thrusts the Word of God against Satan, resists him steadfast, God declares that he will flee. In Heb. 4:12, we are told that the Word of God is powerful, but its power operates only as faith rests upon it. Heb. 4:2 tells us of people who did not profit by the Word of God because they did not mix faith with it. We must so mix faith with the Word of God that we shall not leave any part of that Word upon which we do not rest in faith. God says that man must live by *every word* that proceedeth out of the mouth of God. We are to place our faith on all that God has said and believe it for no other reason than that God Himself has said it.

This exercise of faith is also a means of growth. As we exercise our faith by "mixing" it with all of God's Word, causing our faith to lay hold of the sure foundation—God's promises—the "measure of faith" that God hath given us grows large and strong. In the parable of the talents (Matt. 25:16), the portion that the Lord gave to each man who used it was doubled by his using it. Every day use all the faith that God has given you and see it become twice as much. Faith always pleases God and He says that "without faith it is impossible to please Him." Heb. 11:6. Jesus asked if He would find faith on the earth when He comes. When Satan desired to have Peter, Jesus prayed for only one thing; not that he might have faith, for he already had it, but that his faith might not fail.

We may let our faith fail by not placing it on the Word of God and holding it there, even while Satan contradicts that Word and offers a lie instead. We can let our faith fail by looking at circumstances, conditions, or even at our faith; but our faith will never fail us if we keep our eyes fixed on God, His almightiness, His faithfulness, His sure promises, and His oath to keep every promise He has made. Abraham looked only at the promise of God, and his faith did not fail, but was strong. Jesus will not be satisfied if we continue to have only the amount of faith He at first gave us. In Matt. 25:24-30 the servant who had kept all that the Lord had given him and offered it all back to the Lord was called wicked, slothful, and unprofitable, and was cast into outer darkness because he had not increased the amount the Lord had given. God's command to us is to grow, to increase, and He will expect everything He intrusts us with to enlarge greatly so that when He comes, we can return to Him far more than He gave us. Matt. 25:27 speaks of receiving His own with usury (interest). Another way to make faith grow is to declare it. That is why God says, "Hold fast the profession of your faith." Faith becomes stronger as you say you believe.

Let us see to it that our faith grows by using God's means for growth—feeding constantly on the Word; seeing nothing but God in His almightiness and faithfulness; having for the sure foundation upon which our faith rests, God and His Word; exercising our faith daily and hourly, and also holding fast the profession of it by declaring that we do believe. May God be able to say to each one of us day by day, "Your faith groweth exceedingly."

CHAPTER 18

GREAT REWARD

God says in Heb. 10:35 that He will reward confidence, and it shall not be a small thing, but a *"great recompense of reward"*—words piled upon words to express the greatness of the reward God will give to those who exercise confidence toward Him.

In Heb. 3:6 God tells us what some of the rewards of confidence are. He says we are made the house of Christ if we *continue* in confidence—do not weaken, relax, or let down in it. But He says we must add to it rejoicing. There must be just as much rejoicing as there is confidence.

The Israelites were told to make trumpets of their redemption money and sound these trumpets in the year of Jubilee when every one got all his inheritance back. If ever we get full redemption, we shall have to keep sounding the trumpet of rejoicing. "Rejoice evermore"—all the time.

Jesus will keep His house in good repair. He will not suffer it to be broken by sickness, disease, pain, weakness, or sin. When we are truly, wholly, unreservedly His house, He will keep us free from injury.

In Heb. 3:14 we are told more of the reward God will give for confidence—"We are made partakers of Christ." Made to partake of *His* life, health, strength, vigor, and holiness. One translation says made *partners* of Christ. A partner usually has all the other has, and just as much of it. The Bible says we are joint heirs with Christ—this is partnership. Is not all this truly a *"Great recompense* of reward"? And all this reward is just for confidence. How necessary it is for us to know what confidence is and then to *have* this confidence toward God.

1 John 5:14, 15 tells us that confidence in God is to *know* that we *have* what we asked Him for. Not that we *shall* have it sometime, but that we *do* have it *now.* Not that we hope for it or expect it, but that we *have* it now. How are we to know that we have it? God does not say that we know we have it because we *see* it, *feel* it, or experience it. He tells us how we can *know* that we have it, even if we cannot see it, feel it, or experience it. Sometimes we have these proofs, but sometimes we do not have even one of them, and yet God says we can know, of a certainty, that we do now have the thing for which we asked.

In the first part of the chapter (1 John 5) God has been talking of our being born again and living in full obedience to God. Until we do this we *cannot* have confidence. But in ten minutes we can be born again and can set our hearts to obey God in all things, fully and forever and God will accept the purpose, and then we can have confidence.

In verse 14, He says that what we ask is to be according to God's will. How can we know whether it is according to His will? The Bible is God's *expressed* will. If we ask anything God has promised, it is His will to give it or do it. Meet carefully and fully all the conditions God has given, then ask for the thing, in Jesus' name; and verse 14 says God hears us every time. Here is where the confidence that brings such marvelous rewards assures us that "This thing is promised in His Word and I have met all the conditions and *know* He hears, because He is "faithful that promised." Because He is faithful, *I know I have* the thing He promised, even though I do not see it or feel it.

Heb. 10:35 tells us not to cast away this precious confidence which says, *"I know I have* it." Heb. 3:6 speaks in addition of holding fast "the rejoicing of the hope" and of continuing to exercise equal amounts of confidence, with rejoicing, praising, thanking, and being glad and jubilant *because* we *have* what we asked. Heb. 3:14 warns us not to weaken, relax or let down in the least until the *end* when you can see, feel and use all that confidence has been saying you had.

How it honors God to believe Him when every sense contradicts. God says He will honor those who honor Him, and He does it by making real what you have believed for. One translation of Mark 11:24 is, "When you pray, believe you *have* received what you asked for and you *shall* have it."

This also is confidence—"I *have* it." God's law for every obedient child of His is, *"Be* it unto thee as thou hast believed." Not, be it as you see, feel or experience, but as you *believe*. Confidence says, "I *have* it," and God says, "As thou hast believed, so be it done unto thee" (Matt. 8:13), and the thing is yours. God longs to be believed without proof or evidence. He stands watching, waiting, and the moment He sees that you truly believe, He cries out: "Be it done unto thee," and it is yours.

God will never change this decree nor cease to execute it. Just believe Him and "fight the good fight of faith" by refusing to let one doubt or question enter when Satan brings them up. God says if you waver, you shall not receive *anything at all*. James 1:6, 7. To waver is to wonder, question, doubt, or try to see or feel. To waver not is to see nothing but the almighty, faithful God and His Word and to know that He is faithful, true and unchangeable. *Then* you know that you have that thing for which you asked, and for which you met the conditions. If you have failed God in any way, quickly forsake and confess your failure and claim 1 John 1:9, then all is right.

"Let God be true but every man a liar." Rom. 3:4. Believe God and refuse to believe all that comes from any other person or even from yourself—sight, feeling, experience, reason, and appearances; give the lie to all they say, believe God, and rejoice. Eve fell by disbelieving God and believing her senses—she *saw* that it was *good* and to be *desired*—she believed and followed these, and fell. If we ever fully get back to God, we shall have to reverse the fall—believe God and refuse to believe a single one of our senses or human leadings or wisdom. This is obeying God, calling "those things that be *not* (to all our human senses, understanding and knowledge) as though *they were.*" Rom. 4:17. We shall also have to call the things that are, as though they were not. This is getting out of the natural into the supernatural. "Walk by faith, and not by sight," feeling, sense, or nature. Walk in the Spirit and walk with God. Enoch did it, and his reward was to escape from death. Walk in the narrow way that leads to life—the fullness of life that Jesus came to bring for spirit, soul and body.